one-paragraph recipes
for flavour *without* fuss

RUSTLE UP

Rhiannon Batten
& Laura Rowe

FOR MY MAJA, THE BEST COOK I KNOW.
FOR MARJORIE.

Pavilion
An imprint of HarperCollinsPublishers Ltd
1 London Bridge Street
London SE1 9GF

www.harpercollins.co.uk

HarperCollinsPublishers
1st Floor, Watermarque Building
Ringsend Road Dublin 4
Ireland

10 9 8 7 6 5 4 3 2 1

First published in Great Britain by
Pavilion, an imprint of HarperCollinsPublishers Ltd 2022

Copyright © Rhiannon Batten and Laura Rowe

Rhiannon Batten and Laura Rowe assert the moral right to be identified as the authors
of this work. A catalogue record for this book is available from the British Library.

ISBN 978-1-911682-34-9

MIX
Paper from
responsible sources
FSC® C007454

This book is produced from independently certified FSC™ paper
to ensure responsible forest management.

For more information visit: www.harpercollins.co.uk/green

Printed and bound in China by RR Donnelley APS

Reproduction by Rival Colour Ltd., UK

Photography: Claire Winfield
Food Styling: Lola Milne
Prop Styling: Lauren Miller
Design Manager & Art Direction: Laura Russell
Design: Maeve Bargman
Commissioning Editor: Sophie Allen

CONTENTS

INTRODUCTION

The name of this book didn't take too much debate between us because it's the way we instinctively cook. Sustaining weeknight suppers cajoled from a single pot, sunny weekend brunches, comforting casseroles, quick and easy snacks, and simple, sweet mouthfuls – *Rustle Up* perfectly encapsulates our low-fuss, high-flavour approach to food.

As busy food writers and enthusiastic home cooks, we have discovered the art of the delicious easy life – micro recipes. *Rustle Up* is a collection of our favourite, tried-and-tested recipes; kept short and sweet at just one paragraph each, they promise good food, whether you're cooking in a tiny galley, a shiny, marble-topped kitchen or around a campfire.

These recipes make use of a capsule wardrobe of ingredients, often ones you'll already have in your store cupboard or on fridge shelves. They are those we turn to again and again – because they are powerhouses of flavour and/or texture, and because we passionately care about low-waste cooking. We want to show you the versatility of a pot of thick and tangy Greek yogurt; how a jar of tapenade can be used at breakfast or dinner time; and that Quick-Pickled Onions go with just about anything. It's also for these reasons that, for every recipe throughout the book, we share our top tips and twists.

The tips are those we've learnt from our years in the industry and by cooking for ourselves and our hungry boys (big and small) at home – from clever uses for tinned chickpea water and freezing ginger for easy grating, to seasoning dishes with olive brine. We'll reduce your waste, save you time, and improve your cooking confidence.

The twists will help you really sweat these 104 recipes to make them work for you. Don't have a particular ingredient? No worries, we'll suggest alternatives. Want to make something vegan? We're here for your #meatfreemonday. We've also got ideas for leftovers and pairing suggestions to make the dishes stretch even further.

The chapters are listed in order of when you might like to cook or drink – although the beauty is that most can be cooked and eaten anytime, anywhere.

Stripped back to basics, to maximize your time and minimize confusion, the recipes aren't limited to one pan or a certain number of ingredients and we don't promise ultra-rapid cooking times (although we have listed timings so you can plan your day); but, all are short, simple and manageable. You won't need fancy equipment, or even to have had much practice in the kitchen. There are no rules – just nudges in the right direction. So, whether you're after a solo post-work supper, easy date-night dining, meals with mates or family gatherings, here's to rustling up a storm.

Rhiannon and Laura

'Light-work dishes to make your soul (and stomach) shine'

The great thing about the first meal of the day is the sheer variety it encompasses if you look beyond the usual British suspects of cereal or toast. Here we narrow down the options to dishes that, we promise, will make your morning feel brighter. From a rainbow of prep-ahead smoothies to a cheat's twist on a cinnamon bun, and a chilli-spiked coconut kedgeree for weekend brunches, all are packed with flavour yet short on fuss.

Simple and sustaining, overnight oats are a great alternative to porridge. Adding the apple at the start boosts the flavour and gives the oats a slightly looser texture.

Serves 4 | 10 mins + overnight soaking

APPLE CRUMBLE OATS

Put **200g oats** (choose rolled for a smoother texture or jumbo for a chewier one) in a large bowl with **300ml milk**, **2 apples** (unpeeled and grated) and ½ **tsp mixed spice**. Stir and refrigerate overnight in a sealed container. In the morning spoon into bowls and add **2 tbsp Greek yogurt**, a further dusting of mixed spice and a **thinly sliced quarter of an apple** to each serving.

TWIST

To make this recipe vegan, swap in plant-based milk and coconut yogurt. For extra creaminess try adding a tablespoon of nut butter (smooth or crunchy). If you're not a fan of apples, other good flavour combinations include tahini and dates, or banana with nut butter (a ginger and almond one would work well).

When Rhiannon's friend Mike goes camping he fires up the stove each morning to make his signature 'Best Breakfast in Town'. We couldn't possibly share his closely guarded recipe, but as savoury one-pot breakfasts go, our version is definitely worth getting out of that tent – or bed – for.

Serves 4 | 35 mins

THE BBIT

Warm **1 tbsp vegetable oil** to a medium heat in a large pan. Add **200g smoked bacon** (cut into 1cm strips) and cook until browned. Depending on how fatty the bacon is, add another 2 tbsp oil, **1 finely sliced onion** and **1 diced green pepper** and cook for 5 minutes. Add **250g sliced mushrooms** and cook for a further 10 minutes, stirring every so often. Add **100ml vegetable stock** and **1 x 400g can drained cannellini beans**, turn up the heat and simmer for 5 minutes. Season, add **1 tsp ground cumin** and **200g washed, torn spinach**. Toast **4 slices of bread**. After a few minutes, when the spinach has wilted and any excess liquid has bubbled off, spoon the beans onto the toast and top each one with **finely chopped flat-leaf parsley**.

TWIST

To make this veggie, leave out the bacon and top the beans with 1 tbsp Greek yogurt and a scattering of chilli flakes and za'atar, as well as the flat-leaf parsley.

Pure comfort food – and a good, cupboard-foraging recipe to have on hand when the shelves are getting a bit low on supplies – this home-cooked take on the greasy spoon classic swaps chips for fried potato coins.

Serves 4 | 35 mins | Veggie

SMUDGED EGG AND CHIPS

Heat **2 tbsp olive oil** in a large frying pan over a medium heat. Leaving the skin on, cut **8 medium floury potatoes** into thin coins. Tip into the pan, season and fry for 15–20 minutes, flipping every so often – you may need to do this in batches, depending on the size of your pan. When golden on the outside and soft inside, divide the potatoes between four plates. Add **2 tbsp more oil** and fry **4 eggs**. Place an egg on top of each mound of potatoes. In the empty pan, which should still be coated with oil, fry **12 sage leaves** for a few seconds on each side, blot them on kitchen paper then scatter over the eggs, along with a pinch of **pul biber** or ground black pepper.

TWIST

If you prefer baked potatoes to fried, cut them into wedges, toss them in olive oil and salt and roast in the oven at 180°C fan/200°C/400°F/gas mark 6 for 30 minutes, turning at least once. Sweet potatoes work well, too.

We love fish for breakfast, as anyone who has witnessed us avidly ordering grilled kippers or smoked haddock from a hotel breakfast menu will testify. With spice as well as fish, kedgeree makes a great, taste bud-waking brunch dish.

Serves 4 | 35 mins

CHILLI AND COCONUT KEDGEREE

Heat **1 tbsp vegetable oil** in a large pan and add **1 onion** and **1 green chilli**, both finely chopped. Cook over a medium heat for 5–10 minutes, or until the onion has softened, then add a **thumb of finely diced ginger**, **½ tbsp garam masala** and **1 tsp ground turmeric**. Stir, cook for another minute, then add **200g basmati rice**. Add **1 x 400ml can coconut milk** and **200ml vegetable stock**, stir, bring to a simmer then cover and let it bubble for 15 minutes or until the rice has cooked. Meanwhile, boil **2 eggs** for 6½ minutes then plunge into cold water, peel and quarter. Stir **150g frozen peas** into the cooked rice and warm through, then scatter **150–200g flaked mixed hot-smoked fish** through the rice, season and serve topped with **chopped curly parsley** and the quartered eggs. Stir the **juice of 1 lemon** through **150g plain yogurt** with a good pinch of salt and spoon it onto the side.

TWIST

Try stirring 1 tbsp of lime pickle through the yogurt instead of the lemon juice, or swapping mixed hot-smoked fish for cooked, smoked fish.

The traditional fruit salad has a lot to answer for, but this two-tone variation on the theme is a very different proposition. Blending perfumed melons, nectarines and apricots, it's sticky with juice, crunchy with seeds and rich with flavour.

Serves 4 | 20 mins | Veggie

GREEN AND GOLD SALAD

Heat the oven to 130°C fan/150°C/300°F/gas mark 2, then mix **2 tbsp melted salted butter, 2 tsp caster sugar, ½ tsp ground cinnamon** and **½ tsp ground ginger** in a bowl. Pour in **100g seeds** (try a mix of pumpkin, sunflower and sesame) and stir to coat. Spread the sticky seeds on a baking tray and bake for 10–15 minutes, stirring and turning mid-way through cooking. Allow to cool. Meanwhile, deseed and peel **2 different-coloured melons** (honeydew or galia, plus cantaloupe works well), and stone **2 white nectarines** and **4 apricots**, then cut them all into slices. Arrange on a plate, scattered with **mint leaves** and the **spiced seeds**. Serve with **yogurt**, if you like.

TIP

Slices of melon look prettier but cubes are more transportable if you're making this for a breakfast picnic or lunchbox. Drizzle a spoonful of syrup from a jar of stem ginger over the cubes and stir to coat the fruit.

TWIST

Crunchy toast and cooling,
creamy yogurt is an addictive
brekkie base. Try slow-cooked
cherry tomatoes topped
with Chinese crispy chilli oil,
or fried, crumbled Italian
sausage.

Miso's sweet-savouriness and nutty brown butter is a stellar match for the earthiness of mushrooms. And once you've tried cold, thick Greek yogurt on toast instead of butter, you'll find it hard to go back.

Serves 2 | 15 mins | Veggie

MISO BROWN BUTTER MUSHROOMS

Add **1 tbsp olive oil** to a wide frying pan or wok over a medium-high heat. Add **2 tbsp white miso paste**, stir, then toss in **400g mushrooms** (chestnut and shiitake work well – halved or quartered depending on size) and fry, stirring occasionally to ensure they don't catch or burn, for 10–12 minutes or until any water has evaporated and the mushrooms are sticky and caramelized. Meanwhile, toast **4 sourdough slices** and melt **25g butter** in a separate small pan until it foams, begins to turn a golden brown and smells nutty. Take off the heat. Spread cold, thick **Greek yogurt or labneh** on the hot toast, tip over the mushrooms, season with a pinch of flaky sea salt, if needed, and pour over the browned butter and some **chopped flat-leaf parsley**.

TIP

Labneh is a thing of beauty. Line a sieve with clean muslin or a tea towel, spoon in thick yogurt, loosely cover, place over a bowl and sit in the fridge overnight to drain. You'll be left with thick labneh, which is delicious on its own, or can be rolled into balls and plopped into a large jar of olive oil, herbs and garlic to marinate.

The buttery, warming flavours of a cinnamon bun without any baking, this recipe works with most springy white breads if you can't find a brioche loaf. If you don't have time to stew the apples, try it topped with Greek yogurt and lemon curd.

Serves 4 | 35 mins

CINNAMON BUN TOAST

Melt a **large knob of butter** and **2 tbsp golden caster sugar** in a pan and stir in **6 apples** (peeled, cored and chunkily sliced or diced) and **½ tsp ground cinnamon**. Add a lid and cook over a low-medium heat for 30 minutes. Meanwhile, whip together **4 tbsp softened butter**, **1 tbsp caster sugar** and **1 tsp ground cinnamon**. When the apples are cooked, toast **4 brioche slices**, then spread quickly with the cinnamon butter so it melts. Serve topped with the stewed apples, a final dusting of ground cinnamon and, if you feel like it, a **dollop of Greek yogurt**.

TWIST

It's worth making more butter than you need and baking peaches with the leftovers as a quick pudding. Halve and stone 4 peaches, place them cut-side up in an ovenproof dish, dot 1 tsp of cinnamon-sugar butter into each cavity and bake for 10–15 minutes at 180°C fan/200°C/400°F/gas mark 6.

Tortillas are a great ingredient to have on standby and don't take up much room in the cupboard or freezer. This crunchy burrito is cooked in one pan (no one wants a big wash-up operation) and can be flexed with whatever's in the fridge.

Serves 1 | 5 mins

BREAKFAST BURRITO

Crack **1 egg** into a small bowl and beat with a **splash of milk**. Heat **1 tsp butter** in a frying pan over a medium heat. When the butter begins to foam, pour in the egg and swirl the pan to ensure the whole base of the pan is coated. After 10 seconds, place **a tortilla** on top of the egg. Using a fish slice, apply pressure to the tortilla and after 30–40 seconds, once the egg is just set and stuck to the tortilla, flip the tortilla over. Add **4 slices of Parma ham**, dot over **1 tbsp tapenade** and sprinkle over a **handful of grated Cheddar** down the centre. Fold a third of the tortilla into the middle – it should be golden and crunchy – and then the other. Apply pressure again with the fish slice, before turning out onto a board, and slicing in half.

TWIST

Once you've nailed the egg and tortilla base, you can mix things up with the filling – try slices of chorizo, ham, bacon, salami or avocado; dot over harissa, Potluck Pesto (Hard-Working Recipes, p166), chilli jam, Quick-Pickled Onions (see p167) or sriracha, and sprinkle with grated Manchego, halloumi, Gouda or Emmental.

Whether you divvy up fresh and/or frozen fruit and veg into freezable portions or make yours fresh on the day, these rainbow smoothies will keep you cheery all week. If you're making them for the rest of the family, they easily scale up too.

Each serves 1 | 5 mins

HAPPY DAYS SMOOTHIES

THE BLACK FOREST (Veggie)
Blend **50g frozen cherries, 50g frozen blueberries, 25g frozen raspberries,** ½ banana, **½ tbsp peanut butter, 150g kefir** and ½ **tbsp cacao powder** in a high-power blender until smooth.

THE WIMBLEDON (Veggie)
Blend **100g hulled fresh strawberries, 50g frozen raspberries,** ½ **frozen banana,** ½ **tsp vanilla bean paste,** ¼ **tsp honey** and **100g milk** (dairy or plant-based) in a high-power blender until smooth.

THE GREEN LIST (Vegan)
Blend **1 cored apple, 1 thumb of cucumber, 100g frozen pineapple,** a **frozen cube of spinach,** a **large handful of basil (leaves and stalks)** and some ice in a high-power blender until smooth.

THE TOTALLY TROPICAL (Vegan)
Blend **50g frozen peaches, 25g frozen mango, 25g frozen pineapple,** ½ banana, **150g coconut water** (either left over over from a can of coconut milk or from a carton), **100g water** and the **juice of 1 lime** in a high-power blender until smooth.

BANANARAMA (Veggie)
Blend **1 large frozen banana, 1 tbsp oats, 1 tsp chia seeds, 1 tsp maple syrup, 150g natural yogurt** and a pinch of salt in a high-power blender until smooth.

TIP

For the ultimate blend of temperature and texture, mix fresh and frozen fruit and veg.

Eggy bread is the saviour of a stale loaf, and with these warming spices and fresh, zingy kachumber salad, it will soon become a regular breakfast, lunch or dinner. You may need to fry the bread in batches, depending on the size of your pan.

Serves 2 | 25 mins | Veggie

SPICY EGGY BREAD

Break **4 eggs** into a roasting tin, pour in a **big splash of milk** and whisk well. Add a large pinch of salt, **½ tsp mild curry powder**, **1 tsp garam masala** and **2 tsp hot sauce**. Whisk again, then, using kitchen scissors, snip in a **handful of coriander** and **2 spring onions** and stir before dunking in **4 slices of stale sourdough** or **thick bloomer loaf**. Flip the slices over until they are completely coated and let them soak for 5 minutes. Heat **1 tbsp oil** in a large frying pan with **2 tsp black mustard seeds** and **10 dried curry leaves**. When the seeds start to pop, add the soaked bread slices then pour over any remaining egg, onions and herbs. Fry over a medium heat for 3 minutes or until browned on one side, flip over and repeat. Serve with a **dollop of tomato ketchup** mixed with more hot sauce, and **kachumber**.

TIP

Unless mouldy, never throw away the ends or 'heels' of a loaf. Blitz into breadcrumbs (for the Dukkah-Crusted Chicken on p70) or freeze, ready to fry in olive oil with garlic and/or anchovies and use to top risotto or pasta. Or, chop into croûtons, toss in oil and bake in a hot oven, and use in the Fondue Soup on p34.

Lunch should never be overlooked, in our book. Whether you're packing a lunchbox with leftovers from the night before, making something from scratch during a quick break while working from home, or taking time out to restore and revive over a busy weekend, feed yourself well in the middle of the day and it will help set up your brain and body for a productive afternoon ahead. From simple, nourishing soups to veg-topped tartines, a no-cook mezze and a warming spiced hash, in this chapter you'll find smaller dishes that fit the midday bill perfectly.

This soup is adapted from a childhood favourite of Rhiannon's. Her much-loved Yorkshire granny often seemed to be in the kitchen, with flour on her hands from baking, yet 'cheese and onions' was one recipe that her grandad would commandeer the pinny and pans for. Rich and indulgent, one bowl is all you need.

Serves 4–6 | 25 minutes | Veggie

FONDUE SOUP

Melt **50g butter** in a pan, then add **2 diced onions**, **1 large crushed garlic clove** and **1 tsp salt** and cook gently (lid on) for 10–15 minutes, or until the onions are translucent. Stir in **2 tbsp plain flour** and, when that's absorbed, **150ml acidic white wine** (Picpoul is good), splash by splash, stirring well between each addition. Add **500ml vegetable stock** and simmer on a low heat for 10 minutes. Add **300ml milk** and **250g grated Gruyère** or **strong Cheddar** and heat through, stirring, until the cheese has melted but the soup isn't boiling. Season and blend, adding another tablespoon of flour and cooking until absorbed if you'd rather a thicker consistency. Serve with **Quick-Pickled Onions** (p167) and **toasted breadcrumbs; finely chopped chives** and **sourdough croutons**; or **apple crisps** and **chopped, toasted walnuts**.

TWIST

The soup also makes a good base for an Alpine spin on Welsh rarebit. Add a little more flour to the soup and cook for slightly longer, to thicken it, then spoon onto slices of toast, or baked potato halves, and grill until they're bubbling.

Rye bread gives this classic lunch extra flavour but sourdough works well, too – avoid anything too delicate or your tartine will fall apart. To keep things really simple, just choose one topping.

Serves 4 (2 slices each) | 20 mins | Veggie

GREEN TARTINES

Toast **8 thin slices of rye bread**. Top two with **¼ of a goat's cheese log** (mashed), a drizzle of **extra-virgin olive oil**, **1 tsp pumpkin seeds**, a **couple of basil leaves** and a twist of black pepper. On another two, spread mashed **artichoke hearts (about half a jar)**, a **couple of rocket leaves** and a **couple of shavings of pecorino**. On another two, spread **2 tbsp frozen peas** (brought up to room temperature and mashed with salt and pepper), another **¼ of a goat's cheese log** (sliced), a **drizzle of olive oil**, black pepper and **2 shredded mint leaves**. On the final 2 slices, spread the same mashed pea mixture but top with a **couple of blanched asparagus tips** and a **scattering of chilli flakes**.

TWIST

Try mashed avocado with goat's cheese, radishes and walnuts; or green tomatoes with mozzarella, basil and peppery olive oil. The Loaded Avos combinations on p47 and the Potluck Pesto on p166 would also make great tartine toppings.

Super speedy but packed with flavour, this is a regular school-night supper in Rhiannon's family, and a useful standby on busy evenings. Hold back on the spice paste a little, though, if you're cooking for very young children.

Serves 4 | 30 mins

SPICED SWEET POTATO AND COCONUT SOUP

Heat **1 tbsp vegetable oil** over a low-medium heat in a large saucepan, then add **2 tsp tom yum paste**, stir-fry for a minute then add **1 diced onion** and cook for 8 minutes or so, stirring every now and then until softened. Add **750g sweet potatoes** (around 4–6 peeled and diced) and **700ml vegetable stock** and cook for 20 minutes or so, until the sweet potato is soft. Take off the heat, add **1 x 400ml can coconut milk**, season then blend. Gently reheat, then serve, topped with **chopped coriander**, **Quick-Pickled Onions** (see p167) and **chopped salted, roasted peanuts**.

TIP

Most Thai spice pastes contain fish sauce or dried shrimp, but you can make this soup veggie by swapping in Indian blends, such as korma or tikka masala. Light coconut milk also works fine but instead of buying a product that's been watered down you could mix 1 can of full-fat with 1 can of water and freeze the remainder.

Simple or splendid depending on what your local corner shop keeps in stock –
even the most basic stores sell hummus, olives, cheese, pitta and a chopped salad
– this is the ultimate rustled-up lunch or snacky supper.

Serves 4 | 15 mins | Veggie

CORNER SHOP MEZZE

This dish is all about the arrangement. Start from the centre of the
plate, with a **block of feta** or a **wheel of Camembert**, and work
your way out creatively. To jazz things up a bit, try drizzling the
cheese with **extra-virgin olive oil** and **za'atar** or **honey**, **chilli** and
rosemary (or add those seasonings then bake the cheese in foil for
a few minutes first to make it gooier and fuller-flavoured). Next, add
hummus and **baba ganoush** (sometimes labelled as aubergine dip),
then pile **olives** and a chopped salad (**tomato**, **cucumber** and **onion**
dressed with **extra-virgin olive oil**, **lemon juice**, salt, black pepper
and **flat-leaf parsley)** into the mix. Finally, toast some **pitta** and start
scooping.

TIP

Roasting some quartered tomatoes in olive oil and salt is an easy addition if
you have a bit more time. Save oils and brines to use in other recipes. Olive brine
can be used to salt pasta water and veg, add flavour to sauces, loosen hummus or
added to a martini. Oils can be used in pasta sauces, bean and grain salads and
in salad dressings (Dressy Dressing, p167). Feta brine can be used in pasta sauces
and to marinate chicken.

A good meal for early spring, when your body craves something warm but your lips long for lemony sunshine, this is a meal-in-a-bowl soup. To make it even heartier, serve it with slices of buttered soda bread and a hunk of cheese.

Serves 4 | 35 mins | Vegan

HARICOT BEAN AND LEMON SOUP

Gently heat **1 tbsp olive oil** in a large pan, add **1 diced onion** and cook for around 5 minutes. Add **1 celery stick** and **1 carrot** (both diced), a **sprig of rosemary**, salt and black pepper, and stir. Add **1 litre vegetable stock** and cook for 20 minutes or until the veg has softened but is not complete mush. Add **2 x 400g cans haricot beans** (drained and rinsed) to the pan and warm through. Remove the rosemary stalk (the leaves will have fallen into the soup, which is fine). Scoop out 4 ladles of the soup and blend, then return to the pan along with the finely grated **zest and juice of 1 lemon** and **150g shredded spring greens** or **kale**. Simmer for 5 minutes or until the greens have wilted. Serve drizzled with **extra-virgin olive oil**, **chopped flat-leaf parsley** and **chilli flakes** or **pul biber**.

TWIST

As any baked bean-hating child knows (hello Laura!), beans are so much about texture. We've used haricots here; less powdery than some varieties, they make a really filling soup when whizzed up. For a more broth-like soup, skip the blending.

TWIST

Add ½ tsp hot smoked paprika and 1 tsp hot sauce to the cheese sauce and swap the ham for 'nduja or fried chorizo.

Think of crumpets as flavour sponges – whether for pools of butter and honey (next time try chilli honey), or this version of a French croque madame. Of course, it would work with regular crumpets – but why do things by half?

Serves 3 | 20 mins

CRUMPET CROQUE MADAME

Melt **1 tbsp butter** with **1 tbsp plain flour**, **½ tsp English mustard powder**, **½ tsp ground white pepper** and a pinch of salt in a small pan. Stir for 30 seconds over a low-medium heat, then gradually stir in **100ml whole milk**. Cook for 10 minutes, stirring regularly to ensure it doesn't catch and you have a smooth sauce. Stir in **50g grated Gruyère** and **50g grated Comté** until melted. Meanwhile, toast **3 giant crumpets** under a hot grill, and fry **3 eggs** in **1 tbsp oil**. Spread the toasted crumpets with the cheese sauce, topping each one with a slice of **ham** and a fried egg. As an optional extra, add another handful of grated cheese and grill until melted.

TIP

If you're cooking for guests and want to get ahead, make the cheese sauce up to four days before and keep in the fridge. Spread over hot, toasted crumpets and grill to melt, before topping with ham, fried eggs and cheese.

Put that 1970s classic out of your mind; the loaded avo is worth revisiting, with one simple rule: anything that's crisp, crunchy and fresh makes a winning topping while anything heavy, creamy or rich will be a one-way ticket for your taste buds straight back to the golden age of disco.

Serves 4 (as a starter or part of a mezze-style lunch) | 15 mins

LOADED AVOS

Halve and stone **2 avocados** then fill each cavity with one of four fillings. Into one, add **¾ tbsp extra-virgin olive oil**, **½ tbsp balsamic vinegar**, salt, black pepper and **1 tsp chopped chives**. Fill another with **crumbled feta**, **1 chopped walnut**, **½ a radish** (sliced) and black pepper. Into the third, spoon **2 tbsp chickpeas**, **4 cucumber half-moons**, a **cube of crumbled feta cheese**, **1 tsp Quick-Pickled Onions** (see p166), **½ tsp apple cider vinegar**, **1½ tsp extra-virgin olive oil**, salt and pepper and **1 tsp shredded flat-leaf parsley**. Finally, pile **1–2 tbsp cooked prawns** into the fourth, drizzle with the **zest and juice of ½ lime**, salt and a **few strands of micro-greens** (or flat-leaf parsley).

TWIST

Jazz up avo on toast by topping it with any of the combinations above. Use the Dressy Dressing, from p167, as a quick and easy filling. Use left over walnuts to make Potluck Pesto or Dukkah (p166). Make a salad from left over chickpeas, cucumber, feta, pickled onions and flat-leaf parsley. Use left over prawns in the Prawn Cocktail Grain Bowl on p120.

This fragrant mix of potato, kale and spice sits part-way between the Irish dish, colcannon, and the Indian sabzi or subji. A quick and comforting lunch or tea, topped with thick Greek yogurt and tangy lime pickle, it also makes a good side to roast squash, grilled chicken, or coconut and prawn curry.

Serves 4 | 45 mins | Vegan

SPICED SMASHED HASH

Cut **1kg unpeeled Maris Piper**, **Vivaldi or Désirée potatoes** into eighths, rinse and tip them into a large pan with cold salted water. Cover and bring to the boil then simmer for 20–25 minutes or until cooked, and drain. In another large pan, heat **3 tbsp cold-pressed rapeseed oil** then stir in **1 tsp ground coriander**, **2 tsp ground cumin**, **1 tsp garam masala**, **½ thumb of grated ginger** and **1 tsp black mustard seeds**. When the mustard seeds start to pop, add **1 finely sliced onion** and fry for 5–10 minutes or until softened. Add **200g shredded kale** (any white or green cabbage), **1 tsp salt** and **1 tsp ground turmeric** and stir-fry for a few minutes until the kale has wilted. Tip the potatoes into the pan, stir through the kale, add **2–3 tbsp cold-pressed rapeseed oil**, then roughly mash. Check the seasoning, then speckle with a sliced **red chilli**.

TWIST

Try swapping in other spices (Dijon mustard with chives; paprika with garlic and spring onions) or pairing sweet potatoes with ras el hanout and sliced black olives. If you have hash left over, store it in the fridge; the next day you can mix it with a little flour and a beaten egg to make spiced potato fritters.

Coronation chicken has endured as a sandwich filling and Christmas turkey left over tradition for good reason. This speedy, meat-free version is ideal for a low-fuss lunch and can be spooned into baked potatoes or lettuce cups, spread between thick slices of bread or wrapped in a tortilla with pickled red cabbage.

Serves 2 | 10 mins | Veggie

CORONATION CHICKPEAS

Drain **1 x 400g can chickpeas**, reserving the water (see Hard-Working Recipes on p166). Roughly mash about half, and stir with the remaining whole chickpeas. Add **1 tbsp mango chutney**, **2 tbsp thick Greek yogurt**, the **juice of 1 lime**, **1 tbsp tikka masala curry paste** (or any curry paste that you have), and lots of salt and black pepper. Chop a **handful each of dried apricots and almonds** and stir in, along with a **small handful of chopped coriander leaves**. Spoon into **radicchio leaves**, to serve, if you like.

TWIST

Thinly slice ¼ red cabbage and combine with a pinch of salt, 3 tbsp balsamic vinegar and ½ tsp pomegranate molasses. Wait 20 minutes (or, even better, overnight) before serving alongside the creamy, spicy chickpeas.

Delicious with a salad as a weekend lunch, or sliced up and eaten cold in the week. The beauty of this tart is that it works with most alliums – try different colours and sizes of spring onions, baby leeks, calçots or quartered red or white onions.

Serves 4–6 | 1 hr 15 mins | Veggie

SWEET ALLIUM TART

Heat the oven to 180°C fan/200°C/400°F/gas mark 6. Take **1 garlic bulb** and slice off the top to expose the cloves. Drizzle with **olive oil**, wrap in foil and bake for 40 minutes. Trim the roots and green ends from **2 bunches of spring onions**. Add to a roasting tin, drizzle with **1–2 tbsp olive oil**, sprinkle with salt and roast for 20 minutes. Beat together **180g soft cheese, 1 tsp wholegrain mustard, 1 tsp Dijon mustard, ¼ tsp ground white pepper** and **50g finely grated Parmesan**. Spread out **320g ready-rolled puff pastry** on a lined baking sheet and score a 1cm border. Prick the interior of the border with a fork. Whisk **an egg** with a **splash of milk**, and brush over the pastry. Remove the onions and garlic from the oven and slide in the pastry. Squeeze 3–4 of the softened garlic cloves into the cheese and mustard mix along with any remaining egg wash and stir to combine. Once the pastry is lightly golden (around 20 minutes), remove from the oven and spread the centre with the mustard and garlic mix. Top with the onions and bake for 10–20 minutes or until the filling is set.

TIP

Roasting garlic transforms its flavour and heat, making it sweet and mellow. Squeeze any left over cloves into mayo for a cheat's aioli (see the tip on p85) or beat into butter and spread onto toasted ciabatta for a speedy garlic bread.

This comforting toastie recipe pays tribute to the American Jewish tradition of lox and schmear – a.k.a cured salmon and a spread of soft cheese on a bagel, often served with slices of raw red onion, capers and herbs.

Serves 2 | 15 mins

SMOKED SALMON MELT

Turn on a toastie machine, or place a wide frying pan over a medium heat. Combine **100g soft cheese**, the **zest of 1 lemon**, **¼ finely chopped red onion**, **1 tbsp finely chopped capers**, **1 tbsp finely chopped dill** and **50g chopped smoked salmon**. Butter **4 slices of wholemeal bread** and place 2 of the slices, butter-side down, into the toastie machine or pan. Divide and spread the salmon mix over both slices, sprinkle a **generous handful of grated cheese** over each, and top with the remaining bread slices, butter-side up. If using the toastie machine, toast for double the time it tells you, until crunchy, deeply golden and oozy. If using a pan, place a piece of greaseproof paper on top of the toastie and weigh it down with a plate or another pan and something heavy, like canned tomatoes. Fry until golden and crunchy on one side, turn and repeat.

TIP

This recipe is great for the cheaper cuts of smoked salmon, such as those labelled 'trimmings' or 'ribbons', or with any scrappy bits left at the end of a pack.

Our most enjoyable meals are often around a table. Not the type that involve starched tablecloths or ruler-straight backs but shared meals at kitchen tables among family or friends, ideally with enough time for chairs to be kicked back, candles lit and glasses refilled as the conversation - and the hands of the clock - run on. Food may be the focus of these meals but in a joyful, messy, drips-everywhere kind of way that subtly underpins the pleasure of eating. More often than not the dishes we tend to cook for these comforting, life-affirming meals need no special equipment or expert knowledge.

AROUND THE TABLE

A jewel of a dish, with an intense, romesco-style beetroot sauce, this is great for adding a bit of brightness to midweek mealtimes, and for using up whatever's in the veg box at the end of the week. For variety, try golden or candy beetroot.

Serves 4 | 35 mins | Vegan

RUBY TUESDAY

Heat the oven to 170°C fan/190°C/375°F/gas mark 5. Chop **2 red onions**, **2 beetroot** and **4 red potatoes** (all unpeeled except the onion) into quarters and tip into a baking tin along with **8 whole baby carrots**. Drizzle with **olive oil**, a **handful of thyme leaves** and season, then mix. Spread the veg out into a single layer and roast for 25 minutes. Meanwhile, toast a **couple of handfuls of walnuts** on a baking sheet for around 8 minutes and set aside. After the 25 minutes, remove the beetroot, while the other veg keep cooking. Blend the beetroot with **1 garlic clove, 200g canned chopped tomatoes**, a generous pinch of salt, **2 tsp sherry vinegar**, 6 of the toasted walnuts and **2 tbsp extra-virgin olive oil** and blitz until smooth. Warm the sauce through and serve with the roasted vegetables, crumbling the remaining toasted walnuts and scattering a few more thyme leaves over the top.

TIP

The beetroot sauce is delicious with pasta and as a cold dip with crudites. Use the left over walnuts to make Potluck Pesto or Dukkah – see Hard-Working Recipes on p166.

TWIST

Most root veg can be swapped in, as can cauliflower florets and pumpkin; if you're using the latter, give it an extra 10 minutes or so roasting time before adding the rest of the veg. Or, bulk up the whole dish by serving it on a bed of mixed grains.

This stew packs in masses of flavour with very little effort. It also happens to be an excellent way of using up a bottle of pre-mixed mulled wine if you have some stashed away from Christmas parties past.

Serves 4 | 2 hrs 15 mins

WINTER SOLSTICE STEW

Heat the oven to 140°C fan/160°C/325°F/gas mark 3. In a small pan, bring **75ml bottled mulled wine** to the boil, then reduce the heat and simmer for 10 minutes. Meanwhile, heat **1 tbsp oil** in a heavy-bottomed, lidded pan. Coat **500g diced braising steak** in **2 tbsp seasoned plain flour** and brown in batches in the hot oil. Scoop out onto a plate. Add **2 tbsp olive oil** to the same pan and, over a medium heat, fry **1 finely sliced onion**, **2 sliced carrots**, **2 sliced celery sticks** and **2 bay leaves**, stirring regularly, for around 10 minutes. If the base of the pan is sticking, use 2 tbsp of the mulled wine to deglaze. Return the beef and any of its juices to the pan, along with the reduced mulled wine and **500ml beef stock**. Bring to the boil, then cover and transfer to the oven for 1½–2 hours or until the meat starts to fall apart. Season, sprinkle with **chopped herbs** and serve with **mashed potatoes** or **crusty bread**.

TWIST

Try using venison in place of beef as it's a great way to cook this hearty, flavour-rich meat. Not a fan of carrots? Try turnips or beetroot.

Fennel, fish and cream have been a winning combination for Rhiannon since a trip to Iceland, when a local fisherman cooked her a spectacular, fennel-flecked chowder, topped with tiny fried squid. She's been recreating those flavours in dishes ever since and this is one of her favourites.

Serves 4 | 15 mins

PAN-FRIED SEA BASS WITH FENNEL CREAM

Put a **large knob of butter** in a large frying pan over a gentle heat and, when it starts to bubble, place **4 sea bass fillets** skin-side down and cook for 4 minutes. Add **2 tsp fennel seeds** and cook for another minute. Add **a finely chopped shallot**, **7 tbsp white wine** and **2 tbsp ouzo** or **Pernod** (or skip the spirits and up the wine to 130ml), stir the sauce and turn the fish. Cook for another couple of minutes then add **250ml single cream** (bring it up to room temperature first so it doesn't curdle when it hits the pan) and season generously. Cook for another minute or two, until the cream is just starting to bubble, then serve with **steamed rice** and crisp **green beans**.

TIP

Look out for organically farmed or line-caught sea bass. If you can't find those, whiting, dab and plaice are all good alternatives, as are hake, haddock and coley (though fillets of those last three are thicker so will need a bit longer in the pan).

A spell in Germany left Rhiannon with a soft spot for the country's culinary treasures, among them *Himmel und Erde* – 'Heaven and Earth' – a simple dish of mashed potato and apple that is often served with sausages. Here, it's reimagined as jacket potato hot dogs topped with apple-flecked onions.

Serves 4 | 1 hr 10 mins

HEAVEN AND EARTH HOT DOGS

Heat the oven to 180°C fan/200°C/400°F/gas mark 6. Prick, oil and salt **4 baking potatoes** and cook them in the oven for an hour. Meanwhile, mix together **1 tbsp honey**, **1 tsp wholegrain mustard** and **½ tsp apple cider vinegar**, then pour over **4 pork sausages** in a roasting tin. Roll the sausages to coat them in the glaze, then cook in the oven, beneath the potatoes, for 20–25 minutes, turning and basting them every so often. Melt a **large knob of butter** in a frying pan, toss in **2 thinly sliced onions** and cook for 15 minutes over a low-medium heat, stirring regularly. Add in **1 grated apple** and cook for another 5 minutes then season with salt, black pepper and **1 tbsp thyme leaves**. Slice the potatoes lengthways down the middle, slot a sausage in each one and top with the caramelized onion mix. Serve with **200g watercress**, wilted in a pan with butter, salt and pepper.

TIP

It's worth making double the sweet, caramelized onions. You can then use any spare to turn basic cheese on toast into an appley Welsh rarebit, or add in chopped thyme or sage to make posh cheese toasties.

As with chicken, pork can take strong flavours – especially when it's undercut by a rich, honeyed sweetness. For ultimate success buy the best-quality loin steaks you can and don't be tempted to overcook them.

Serves 4 | 35 mins

MISO SESAME PORK WITH COCONUT GREENS

Place **4 pork loin steaks** in a roasting tin. Mix **50g red miso paste**, **1 tbsp soy sauce**, **1 tbsp honey** and **2 tbsp toasted sesame oil** and coat the meat with it, pouring any leftovers into the roasting tin. Leave this to marinate while you heat the oven to 180°C fan/200°C/400°F/gas mark 6. Place **30g sesame seeds** on a plate, roll the pork steaks in the seeds, then return to the roasting tin and cook for 20 minutes or until just cooked, turning and basting them after 10 minutes. Meanwhile, cook some **rice**. In another pan, heat **3 tbsp coconut oil**, **1 tsp salt** and **2 tsp Chinese five spice** in a frying pan. Add **400g chopped chard** and stir-fry for a couple of minutes. Place the pork steaks, either whole or cut into strips, on the rice with the greens on the side.

TWIST

The coconut chard works with different greens and many Asian spice blends. Try switching out the Chinese five spice with garam masala but bear in mind that five spice is a fairly gentle flavouring; with the more potent, or fiery, spice blends you'll need to use less.

A summery twist on the social media superstar 'baked feta pasta', this dish is pure sunshine in a bowl thanks to vibrant lemon zest and yellow courgettes. Here, we've swapped feta for Wootton White, a favourite Greek-style sheep's cheese from Somerset, but it will work just fine with feta and green courgettes.

Serves 4 | 45 mins | Veggie

SUNSHINE PASTA

Heat the oven to 180°C fan/200°C/400°F/gas mark 6. Cut **3 soleil (yellow) courgettes** into thin diagonal slices and place in a large baking dish. Drizzle with **olive oil**, season and toss to combine. Make a well in the centre of the dish and place a **200g block of Wootton White** or **feta** there. Drizzle the cheese with more oil and plenty of pepper then cook for 25–35 minutes, or until the cheese is soft and wobbly and the courgettes are cooked. While that's baking, cook 2 handfuls of **pasta** per person (conchiglie is good as it makes delicious little pockets of cheese and courgette) in boiling salted water until al dente. Drain, reserving a mug of pasta water. When the cheese and courgettes are cooked, tip the drained pasta into the dish with a couple of tablespoons of the pasta water and stir everything to combine. Sprinkle over the **zest of 1 lemon** and a **handful of basil leaves** and divide between four bowls.

TWIST

Instead of the courgettes, roast some butternut squash on its own for 20 minutes or so before adding the cheese, and swap lemon and basil for honey and sage.

A nut and spice mix originating in Egypt, dukkah can be used to add crunch to traybakes, as a savoury snack (tip some into olive oil then dip pieces of bread into it), as a topping for soups or, as here, to elevate everyday dishes.

Serves 4 | 30 mins

DUKKAH-CRUSTED CHICKEN

Mix **2 tbsp olive oil**, the **zest of 1 lemon, 1 crushed garlic clove** and **1 tsp pomegranate molasses** in a bowl. On a plate mix **2 tbsp dukkah** (see Hard-Working Recipes on p166), **75g breadcrumbs** and salt and pepper. Flatten **4 skinless chicken breasts** to around 1cm thickness (cover with greaseproof paper and bash with a rolling pin), dip them in the oil mixture then coat them in the dukkah mix. Heat **1 tbsp olive oil** in a large frying pan and fry the chicken over a low-medium heat for 6–8 minutes on each side, checking every so often to make sure the breadcrumbs aren't catching. Divide **150g rocket, ½ cucumber**, sliced into thin half-moons, and a **handful of finely chopped flat-leaf parsley** between four plates. Drizzle **2 tbsp olive oil**, the **juice of the zested lemon** and salt and black pepper over the top of the salad and serve with the chicken.

TWIST

For a heartier version of this dish, swap out the salad for rice cooked in stock then added to stir-fried kale with lemon juice and chopped flat-leaf parsley.

Inspired by the recipe in Nigella's book *Cook, Eat, Repeat* for Fish Finger Bhorta (a dish itself inspired by journalist Ash Sarkar's nostalgic take on the Bangladeshi answer to mash), we agree that the British freezer classic is ripe for a reinvention.

Serves 4 | 25 mins

SALT AND PEPPER FISH FINGERS

Heat the oven to 200°C fan/220°C/425°F/gas mark 7 and cook **12 fish fingers** for 20 minutes. In a bowl, mix **2 grated garlic cloves**, a **thumb of grated ginger**, **1 sliced spring onion**, **½ tsp salt** and several grinds of black pepper, **½ deseeded and finely chopped red chilli**, **1 tbsp vegetable oil** and **1 tsp sherry vinegar**. Tip into a large frying pan and cook over a medium heat for 5 minutes. When the fish fingers are cooked, break them up with a spatula and add them to the pan to combine with the aromatics. Serve with **steamed rice** and **broccoli**.

TIP

As food and drink pairings go it may sound an unusual one but fish fingers make a great match with dry Fino and Manzanilla sherries. Think tapas, and how the crisp, almondy flavours cut through the oiliness of fried fish, and give it a go.

Salty, sweet and sticky, this easy baked chicken recipe is just the thing if you've fallen into a midweek meal rut. The ketchupy sweetness of the glaze is spiked with mustard and ginger, then diffused by nutty brown rice and crunchy spring onions.

Serves 4 | 55 mins

STICKY CHICKEN

Heat the oven to 170°C fan/190°C/375°F/gas mark 5. Pat **8 chicken thighs** (skin-on and bone-in) dry. Combine **3 tbsp kecap manis**, **1 tbsp rice wine vinegar**, **½ thumb of grated ginger**, **1 tsp English mustard powder**, **1 grated garlic clove** and **1 tbsp oil** and coat the chicken with the glaze. Bake in the oven for 45 minutes, basting halfway through with the marinade while it cooks. Meanwhile, cook **200g brown rice** in boiling, salted water for 25 minutes, drain and mix in **2 chopped spring onions**, **2 tbsp soy sauce** and the **juice of 1 lime**. Serve the chicken on the rice with any juices spooned over and a **sprinkling of chopped coriander leaves** and **sesame seeds.**

TIP

As an alternative to rice, the chicken also goes well with the Confetti Coleslaw (see p96) and/or with noodles.

This hard-working tomato and chickpea broth can be eaten as a soup, or adapted to make a pasta sauce, a quick veggie curry or a warming merguez stew.

Serves 8 | 30 mins | Vegan

BASE CAMP STEW

Heat **2 tbsp olive oil** in a large pan. Add **4 finely chopped celery sticks**, **2 large crushed garlic cloves**, **1 small deseeded and finely chopped red chilli** and **1 large diced onion**. Cook for 10 minutes or until the onion and celery have softened, then add **2 x 400g cans drained and rinsed chickpeas** and season generously. Add **2 x 400g cans chopped tomatoes** and **1 litre vegetable stock** and bring to a simmer for 10–20 minutes or until thickened. Add **4 handfuls of chopped spinach** and cook until wilted. Serve half the stew now, with **crusty bread**, as a soup, topped with **sliced spring onions** and **coriander leaves**, or **Quick-Pickled Onions** (see p167). Keep the second half for the following day and cook it one of the following three ways.

TWIST 1

Blitz the stew with a blender to make a simple sauce for pasta. Serve it topped with grated cheese and basil.

TWIST 2

Add 1 x 400ml can coconut milk, ½ thumb of grated ginger, 1 tsp ground cumin and 1 tsp garam masala and serve with steamed rice as an easy veggie curry.

TWIST 3

Mash the chickpeas a little to give the stew a bit more body but don't blitz the whole thing. Slice in some grilled merguez sausages and serve with crusty bread.

Packed with flavour and goodness, this dal can be adapted to whatever you have in your veg box or fridge. A grater attachment on a food processor makes speedy work of the veg, but a standard box grater also works fine.

Serves 4 | 50 mins | Vegan

VEG BOX GRATER DAL

Grate **1 onion**, **1 deseeded pepper** (any colour), **2 carrots**, **2 garlic cloves**, a **couple of fistfuls of root vegetables** (celeriac, turnips, swede, beetroot and parsnips) **and/or squash** (butternut, pumpkin) and pop in a large pan with **250g red lentils**, **1 tbsp ground turmeric**, **2 tsp pav bhaji masala** (or any Indian spice blend), **½ tsp ground black pepper**, **2 tsp salt** and **1 dried chilli**. Tip in **1 x 400ml can coconut milk** and another 1½ cans of cold water (use the empty can to measure). Stir, then simmer for 40 minutes over a low-medium heat, stirring regularly. Just before serving, melt **1 tbsp coconut oil** or **groundnut oil** in a small pan, add **1 tsp black mustard seeds** and **10 dried curry leaves**. Fry until fragrant, then pour over the dal to serve.

TWIST

Want to add more to your bowl? Boil or fry eggs and sprinkle with chilli flakes. Or, combine a handful of trimmed chicken livers, 1 tbsp garam masala, 1 tbsp groundnut oil and 1 tsp salt. Fry in a hot pan for 1 minute on each side.

TIP

Orzo, cooked this way,
easily overcooks -
so only make what
you need and eat
immediately!

Orzo risotto doesn't have quite the same al dente bite as regular risotto rice. Adding crunchy breadcrumbs and seeds is a delicious way to break up the soft and creamy texture of this vividly coloured midweek dinner.

Serves 4 | 30 mins | Veggie

KERMIT RISOTTO

Gently fry **1 finely diced red onion** in **1 tbsp olive oil** for 15 minutes or until translucent and softened. Grate in **2 garlic cloves**, stir for a minute, then tip in **400g orzo**, pour over **1 litre vegetable stock**. Simmer and stir regularly. Into a blender, add a **large handful of frozen peas**, a **handful of pumpkin seeds**, a **handful of herbs** (whatever you have but dill, parsley and tarragon work well), **2 tbsp Greek yogurt**, the **juice of ½ lemon**, a slosh more boiling water and a large pinch of salt and blitz until smooth. When the orzo is just al dente and most of the water is absorbed, stir in the pea purée along with a **handful of grated Parmesan** and black pepper.

TWIST

For a crunchy topping, add a handful of breadcrumbs, 1 tbsp olive oil, a bashed unpeeled garlic clove, 1 tbsp pumpkin seeds and salt to a separate pan and fry for 5 minutes until everything is golden.

There can't be a more satisfying signifier you're on a British seaside holiday than chomping into a crab sandwich. This speedy seafood dinner is a nod to this most simple of traditions – ideal for getting into the holiday spirit at any time.

Makes 2 pizzas | 15 mins

PINCER PIZZA

Heat the oven to its hottest setting, and place 2 flat baking sheets on the middle shelves. Mix **140g crème fraîche**, the **juice of 1 lemon**, **25g finely chopped chives**, **½ tsp cayenne pepper**, **65g grated Double Gloucester**, **100g crab meat** (50:50 white and brown is best), and a pinch of salt. Sprinkle **1 tbsp of semolina** or **plain flour** on a sheet of baking paper and roll out 2 balls of **ready-made pizza dough**. Place the pizza bases and baking paper onto the hot trays, spread with the crab mix and bake for 8–10 minutes or until the crust is golden and crisp and the crab is caramelized and bubbly. Sprinkle with extra chopped chives, if you like.

TIP

To really get in the seaside mood, serve with a hazy shandy bass by topping half a glass of real ale with cloudy lemonade. The Italians are partial to a shandy too – there, as in France, it's called panaché – so it's a fitting choice with pizza.

Using ingredients classically associated with the south of France, these bouncy fishcakes take inspiration from Thai cuisine. They are equally delicious served hot for dinner or cold, in a leftovers lunch, the following day.

Serves 4 | 30 mins

TUNA NIÇOISE FISHCAKES

Use a food processor to blend **2 shallots** and the **juice of ½ lemon**. Add **220g raw tuna**, **1 egg**, **1 tbsp tapenade** and a pinch of salt. Pulse until it turns to a sticky paste. Stir in **2 tbsp chopped flat-leaf parsley**, and a **handful each of chopped green beans**, **pitted black olives** and **cherry tomatoes**. Chill the mix for 15 minutes. Meanwhile, boil **300g new potatoes** and **4 eggs**. Heat **5 tbsp olive oil** in a large frying pan until hot then drop spoonfuls of the fishcake mixture, a few at a time (condensing them with the palm of your hand and the spoon before you drop, for a neater shape), into the pan and shallow fry for 30 seconds on each side or until golden and firm. Drain and toss the potatoes with **1 tbsp extra-virgin olive oil**, **1 tbsp chopped fennel fronds** or **dill** and **1 tbsp lemon juice**. Peel and quarter the eggs and serve with the fishcakes and potatoes alongside **lettuce** dressed in more lemon and olive oil or the **Dressy Dressing** (see p167).

TIP

Mix 3 roasted garlic cloves with 5 tbsp mayonnaise for a cheat's aioli to serve alongside the fishcakes.

This recipe first came about when Laura had left over Caesar salad dressing and a hunk of cabbage lurking in the fridge. The bitterness of the cabbage worked so well with the salty punch of the anchovies and Parmesan, it's become a staple.

Serves 4–6 | 20 mins

CURLY CAESAR PASTA

Bring a large pan of salted water to the boil. Meanwhile, in a large bowl, combine **1 finely grated garlic clove, 1 tsp Dijon mustard, 5 finely chopped anchovies** and **1 tsp of the anchovy oil, 50g finely grated Parmesan, 150ml double cream, 1 tbsp lemon juice** and a big pinch each of flaky sea salt and ground black pepper. Add **400g fusilli lunghi** to the boiling water and cook for 8 minutes or until just al dente. Finely shred **1 savoy cabbage**, add to the pan and cook for a further minute, before draining – reserve a cup of the pasta water. Return the drained pasta and cabbage to the pan, add the dressing with a slosh or two of pasta water (it will make your sauce silky smooth) and toss with tongs to combine for 1 minute. Divide between bowls and top with more grated Parmesan.

TWIST

You don't *need* to buy specific shapes but curly pasta really does look great alongside the curly cabbage and it traps all of the delicious sauce – look out for fusilli lunghi, campanelle and mafaldine. Add crispy bacon, too, if you like.

A tiger-striped, pearlescent beauty, we'd happily eat mackerel grilled or baked with nothing more than salt and pepper and a squeeze of lemon. Its strong, rich flavour can also take a punchy, aromatic marinade, like the one in this simple traybake.

Serves 4 | 25 mins

TOM YUM MACKEREL TRAYBAKE

Heat the oven to 180°C fan/200°C/400°F/gas mark 6. Mix **6 tbsp vegetable oil** with **2 tbsp tom yum paste**, the **juice of 1 large lemon**, **1½ tsp sesame seeds** and a pinch of salt and ground black pepper. Make some slits on both sides of **4 whole mackerel** (gutted and cleaned) then place them in a large roasting tin, interspersed with **200g long-stemmed broccoli**, and pour over the tom yum mix, pushing some of it into the slits in the mackerel. Roast for 20 minutes, turning the fish halfway through, while you cook some **rice**. Serve the baked fish and veg beside the rice, drizzling any remaining cooking juices over the top.

TIP

For an extra flavour hit, try stirring 4 tbsp desiccated coconut and the zest and juice of 1 lime through your pan of rice just before you serve.

While you might find DIY XO recipes, they rarely taste as good as the ones made by experts, with the right dried shrimp and scallops, Jinhua ham, chilli, onion and garlic. Buy it online or in Asian grocers and let it do all the heavy lifting.

Serves 4 | 30 mins

XO SWEDE STIR-FRY

Add **1 tbsp groundnut oil** to a wok over a high heat. Add a quartered **red onion** and toss until browned. Add ½ **swede**, peeled and chopped into small bite-sized pieces, and toss for another few minutes or until starting to brown. Add **1 grated garlic clove**, stir-fry for a minute then add 200ml water. Cover the wok and boil furiously for 10–15 minutes, or until the swede is nearly cooked. Add ½ **tsp Chinese five spice**, **200g chopped marinated** or **smoked tofu** and **1 tbsp oyster sauce**. Stir-fry for another 2 minutes, before tossing through **3 tbsp XO sauce** (or 2 tbsp more oyster sauce) and ½ **tsp fish sauce** to season. Serve tossed through **noodles** or alongside **ginger rice** (see below).

TWIST

Instead of noodles, boil 2 cups of basmati rice with 5 cups of water and a large pinch of salt. Boil for 10 minutes or until the water has evaporated and the grains look just cooked. Turn off the heat, cover and leave to steam for 10 minutes. Fluff with a fork before spooning into bowls. Grate a thumb of ginger and mix with 4 tbsp mirin and 2 tbsp rice vinegar. Fluff the rice with a fork, then pour the sauce over it.

TIP

Ginger is best grated
frozen, straight from
the freezer, skin and all.
Just pop any leftovers
back in the freezer when
you're done.

Inspired by penne alla vodka, this one-pot recipe uses store cupboard ingredients and only takes half an hour to prepare. All of the magical starch water is saved, making it beautifully creamy.

Serves 2 | 30 mins | Veggie

SCHOOL-NIGHT ONE-POT PASTA

Warm **4 tbsp olive oil** in a large, deep-sided, heavy-bottomed frying pan over a low-medium heat. Meanwhile, finely slice **4 shallots** and add to the pan with a pinch of flaky sea salt. Stir and cook for 5–8 minutes or until soft and golden. Add **4 finely sliced garlic cloves**, cook for a further minute, then add **4 tbsp tomato purée**, **1 tsp chilli flakes** and **50ml vodka** (optional). Cook, stirring regularly, for 3–4 minutes. Add **300g pasta** to the pan along with 900ml boiling water. Stir, turn up the heat to high, add salt and black pepper and allow to boil for 8–10 minutes or until the pasta is cooked and the water has reduced to a sauce. Stir occasionally, to ensure the pasta doesn't catch. Turn off the heat, and leave to rest for a few minutes, before stirring in **2 tbsp mascarpone**. Season and serve with a cloud of **grated Parmesan** and extra chilli flakes, if you like.

TIP

A heavy-bottomed, cast-iron pan is ideal for one-pot pasta as the heat distribution helps the pasta cook evenly with the sauce. If you don't have shallots, and want to use onions instead, you'll need to cook them for longer to ensure they're softened, sweet and just golden – allow 20–25 minutes.

There are very few meals that aren't improved by adding in some salad, whether as a bright, leafy side to a creamy gratin, a citrus-spritzed chaser to a hearty winter stew, or as a rainbow-hued main event. Here are some of our favourites, from a filling pasta salad full of crunch and zing, to a summery smooshed tomato side and a warm coconut salad that's perfect for rebooting the senses.

For speed in this colourful salad, we suggest chopping the veg in batches in a food processor with the S-blade. If you prefer a shredded coleslaw, use a shredder blade, or finely slice the cabbage and spring onion and grate the carrot by hand.

Serves 4 | 20 mins | Veggie

CONFETTI COLESLAW

Lightly toast **25g salted peanuts** in a pan, cool slightly then pulse in a food processor and set aside. Peel and roughly chop **2 large carrots**, **2 spring onions**, **½ small red cabbage** and **½ small white cabbage**. Working in handful-sized batches, blitz the veg in a food processor, tipping the 'confetti' into a large bowl and mixing everything together as you go. In a jug, mix **5 tbsp toasted sesame oil**, **3 tbsp soy sauce**, **1 tbsp honey** and **3 tbsp lime juice** and, when combined, pour over the coleslaw. Stir to combine then spoon the coleslaw into four bowls, shower with a handful of **finely chopped coriander leaves**, and top with the peanuts and some sliced **radishes**.

TIP

To make this vibrant salad (and the Shelfie Salad on p99) vegan, use maple syrup or your favourite plant-based sweetener instead of the honey.

TWIST

Turn the coleslaw into an easy lunch or dinner by cooking 4 nests of soba noodles then plunging them into cold water. Let them cool for a minute or so, then drain and stir through the coleslaw to serve as a cold noodle salad, topping with the finely chopped coriander, peanuts and sliced radishes.

This is a great way to use up whatever is in the cupboard and fridge – a versatile 'anything goes' kind of recipe. For ultimate ease leave the skin on when roasting the squash but if you prefer it without peel the skin before roasting.

Serves 4 | 50 mins | Veggie

SHELFIE SALAD

Heat the oven to 180°C fan/200°C/400°F/gas mark 6. Cut a **butternut squash** in half lengthways and scoop out the seeds. Slice into 2cm pieces, place on a baking tray and drizzle with **olive oil**, salt and pepper. Roast for 30–40 minutes or until soft and caramelized. Meanwhile, roast **4 tbsp hazelnuts** on a separate baking tray for 8–10 minutes, then cool slightly and bash them. Divide **180g mixed leaves** between four bowls. Combine **4 tbsp tahini**, **3 tbsp olive oil**, 2 tbsp cold water, the **juice of 1 lemon**, **1 tsp honey** and salt and black pepper. Arrange the cooked squash on the leaves, drizzle with the tahini dressing, scatter with the nuts and shower with a **handful of chopped mint leaves**.

TWIST

Think of this as a salad in four layers and get creative. Start with lettuce or greens. Add a core ingredient (we've used butternut squash but try roast aubergine, cauliflower or sweet potatoes, cooked green lentils, grilled salmon, warmed halloumi or falafel). Drizzle with the dressing (or switch to Dressy Dressing, p167). Then top with nuts, seeds, chopped spring onions and fresh herbs.

Simple but delicious, the trick with this recipe is to pick a watermelon so ripe it's full of sweet, rich juice. This is one to eat right away; try to keep some for a next-day lunch box and you'll find yourself with soggy pitta.

Serves 4 | 10 mins | Veggie

WATERMELON AND FETA PANZANELLA

Finely slice ¼ **red onion** and mix with **2 tbsp balsamic vinegar, 6 tbsp extra-virgin olive oil** and black pepper in a large bowl. Add a **medium-sized watermelon** (cut into bite-sized cubes) and stir. Add **200g double-toasted pitta**, broken into bite-size pieces, and stir again. Crumble over **180g room-temperature feta** and a generous **handful of chopped basil leaves**. Stir again, season and serve.

TWIST

Fruit and cheese make good foundations for salads. Good combinations include pear and creamy blue cheeses with chicory or radicchio; crisp apples and sharp, Cheddars with mustardy dressings; and crumbly Lancashire or Wensleydale with ripe nectarines and the Dressy Dressing (see p167) would work really well with this.

From buttered spring greens to Christmassy red cabbage, cabbage can do no wrong in our kitchens. If you're yet to be convinced of the brassica's charms, give this warm salad a go – a twist on thoran, a dry Keralan curry, but with lime, mirin and fish sauce in place of the more traditional South Indian spices.

Serves 4 | 20 mins

WARM COCONUT SALAD WITH TURMERIC EGGS

Place **100g desiccated coconut** in a heatproof bowl and cover with boiling water. Heat **2 tbsp vegetable oil** in a wok. Toss in a **thumb of grated ginger**, **1 grated garlic clove**, **2 tbsp fish sauce**, **1 tbsp mirin**, **1 small, finely sliced red chilli** and stir-fry for a minute. Add **½ finely shredded savoy** or **sweetheart cabbage**, **2 grated carrots** and **2 large, finely sliced leeks**, plus the **juice of 1 lime** and stir-fry for another 5 minutes or until the veg have softened. Meanwhile, heat **2½ tbsp vegetable oil** in a separate frying pan, add **½ tsp ground turmeric** and, when it's hot, crack in **4 eggs,** spooning the oil over them as they cook for 2–3 minutes. Drain the coconut and add it to the cabbage, along with a **handful of chopped coriander leaves**. Stir, then spoon the spiced cabbage onto plates. Place an egg on top of each one, season and sprinkle with more chopped coriander, some **Quick-Pickled Onions** (see p167) and some **chilli flakes**.

TWIST

Left over salad can be used as a filling for a lunchtime wrap the following day; add some plain yogurt, aubergine pickle and a squeeze of lime juice for good measure. To make it veggie, swap the fish sauce for tamari.

The dressing on this salad is a homemade take on the salad sauces and creams popularized by Eliza Acton and Mrs Beeton (and, later, one Henry Heinz). A summer staple of Rhiannon's much-loved great aunt, who grew up on a Wensleydale farm, it has become a favourite in her own home.

Serves 4 (as a side) | 5 mins | Veggie

FARMHOUSE SALAD

In a large bowl whisk together **2 tbsp caster sugar, ½ tsp English mustard powder**, a pinch of salt, 3 pinches of black pepper, **4 tbsp single cream** and **2 tbsp apple cider vinegar** until smooth. Add a **whole torn lettuce** (butterhead, oakleaf, batavia or round lettuce are best), **4 chopped mint leaves** and **2 finely sliced spring onions** and toss to combine. If you have some **flowering chives**, snip those up and scatter them over the salad too (optional).

TIP

The modest-sounding ingredients here perform a culinary magic when mixed together. Despite the cream this is a very light dressing, not at all like a classic salad cream, though you can swap the cream for 2 tbsp Greek yogurt and 2 tbsp buttermilk and leave out the sugar if you like. Alternatively, try the Dressy Dressing (see p167).

More usually served with grilled or barbecued meats, the Argentinian sauce chimichurri also makes an excellent condiment for roast veg. Traditionally made with herbs and chilli flakes, our version uses rose harissa. This doesn't turn the chimi pink but it does give it an extra, slightly smoky, depth of flavour.

Serves 4 | 35 mins | Veggie

ROAST CARROTS WITH ROSY CHIMI

Heat the oven to 180°C fan/200°C/400°F/gas mark 6. Trim then cut **16 medium carrots** in half, place on a baking tray, drizzle with **olive oil**, salt and pepper and roast for 30 minutes or until tender, turning them over after 15 minutes. Meanwhile, spread a **couple of handfuls of walnut halves** on a separate baking tray and toast in the oven for 8–10 minutes, then remove and allow to cool a little. Make the rosy chimichurri by blitzing together a **large bunch of flat-leaf parsley**, **1 garlic clove**, **1 shallot**, **1 tsp rose harissa**, **4–5 tbsp extra-virgin olive oil**, the **juice of ½ lemon**, **2 tbsp apple cider vinegar** and salt and black pepper in a food processor – don't overdo it: you want it to look chopped rather than puréed. Divide the cooked carrots between four plates, crumble over **100g goat's cheese**, top with the walnuts, slightly broken up, and drizzle with the chimichurri. If your carrots came with the tops still attached, scatter a few fronds over the sauce.

TWIST

Try swapping the chimichurri for pesto (see Potluck Pesto, p166) or green hummus; put 1 tbsp olive oil, a large bunch of flat-leaf parsley (or carrot tops), 400g chickpeas, 1 tsp za'atar, ½ tsp ground cumin, 1 tsp salt, 1 garlic clove, 2 tbsp tahini and the juice of a lemon in a food processor and blitz. If it's too thick, add 1–2 tbsp cold water.

With a bit of crunch to the potatoes and no mayo, this is a world away from traditional potato salads. Add a green salad and you've got an easy lunch. Or, serve it as a side dish to meat or fish.

Serves 4 | 45 mins | Vegan

HOT POTATO SALAD

Cut **600g waxy potatoes** into 5mm-thick slices (halve them if large) and rinse them. Heat **1 tbsp rapeseed oil** in a large frying pan and add the potatoes, tossing them to coat. Stir-fry for 5 minutes then add 4 tbsp water and steam-fry them (lid off) for 30 minutes or until golden and crisp. Add more water if it evaporates before the potatoes have softened, and carefully flip the potatoes every so often so they don't stick, although flavour, not perfection, is the aim here. When cooked, toss through the **juice of ½ lemon**, a **handful each of chopped flat-leaf parsley** and **chives** (flowers and all if they have them), **½ tbsp drained and chopped capers** (optional), **1 small finely chopped shallot** and a generous amount of salt and black pepper.

TWIST

If new potatoes are in season, steam them instead of frying and toss them in the dressing for a lighter, but still warm, potato salad.

TIP

Try Désirée potatoes, if you can get hold of them – their red skins make this simple dish look extra pretty.

Rhiannon's friend Ella is brilliant at creating dishes that are big on flavour but low on faff. This adapted version of Ella's duck and mango salad has become one of Rhiannon's go-to summer recipes. The duck absorbs the dressing beautifully.

Serves 4 | 4 hrs

DUCK AND PEACH SALAD

Heat the oven to 160°C fan/180°C/350°F/gas mark 4. Pat dry a **whole duck** and prick the skin with a fork. Rub the duck all over with salt and transfer it to the trivet of a roasting tin. Roast for 1 hour then drain off the fat (see Tip), reduce the temperature to 120°C fan/140°C/275°F/gas mark 1 and roast for a further 2½ hours. When the cooking time is nearly up, wash and dry a **head of batavia** or **butterhead lettuce** and tear it into a large bowl. Leave the duck to rest for 15 minutes then shred the meat with a fork. While the duck rests, stone and slice **2 ripe peaches** and scatter them over the lettuce. Make a dressing with **2 tbsp toasted sesame oil**, **4 tbsp soy sauce**, **2 tbsp honey** and the **zest and juice of 2 limes**. Dress the salad and toss the duck meat through it then divide between four bowls and top with **mint leaves**.

TIP

Pour the rendered duck fat into a jam jar, cool then store in the fridge for cooking roast potatoes another day. Double the quantity of dressing and you can store half in the fridge for making Confetti Coleslaw (see p96) later in the week.

This unapologetically loud mash-up of all of Laura's favourite ingredients is addictively creamy, crunchy, sweet, sour, salty and hot – a.k.a seriously sexy. Dial up or down the volume to your taste. It's great on the side of burgers or bangers.

Serves 6–8 as a side | 20 mins | Veggie

SEXY PASTA SALAD

Put a large pan of salted water on to boil. In a large bowl combine **3 tbsp mayonnaise, 1 tbsp tomato ketchup, 4 finely chopped gherkins, 80g finely chopped pickled onions, 4 finely chopped pickled chillies** or **pickled walnuts, 2 finely sliced spring onions, 1 tsp mustard** (any sort will do), **2 tsp hot sauce**, 1 large pinch of flaky sea salt and ½ **tsp ground white pepper**. Once the water is boiling, add **300g short pasta** and **4 large eggs**. Scoop out the eggs after 8 minutes (you're after medium-boiled yolks) and drain the pasta after a further 2–3 minutes (you want it al dente). Run the drained pasta under cold water until the pasta is completely cool and no shapes are sticking together. Add to the salad bowl. Peel the eggs and roughly chop, and toss everything together until well combined. Check for seasoning and serve.

TIP
Make easy work of peeling eggs by tapping the tops and bottoms on a flat surface, before tapping the sides and peeling directly under cold running water.

TIP

Use a mandoline or a food processor to make light work of slicing the crunchy veg.

When it's warm outside, there's little better than cold, crunchy veg and a cool, creamy dressing made with gut-friendly kefir and cider vinegar. Add in the aniseed flavour of fennel and tarragon, sweet-sharp apple and smoky protein, and you'll find it hard to bump this off your regular recipe rota.

Serves 2–3 | 15 mins

KOHLRABI, KEFIR AND SMOKED TROUT SALAD

Finely grate **1 small garlic clove** into a large bowl. Add **1 tbsp drained and chopped capers**, **2 finely diced shallots**, a **handful of tarragon leaves** (stripped and chopped), **8 tbsp plain kefir**, **1 tsp Dijon mustard**, **1 tbsp apple cider vinegar** and a big pinch of flaky sea salt. Whisk together to combine. Finely slice ½ **kohlrabi**, ½ **cucumber**, ½ **fennel** and **1 crisp, sweet apple**. Add to the bowl, and tear in **6 romaine lettuce leaves**. Toss together, ensuring everything is coated in dressing, before flaking in **125g hot-smoked trout** and giving another gentle toss.

TWIST

Swap the smoked trout for slices of hot-smoked salmon, smoked chicken, smoked Cheddar or smoked mackerel. Try yogurt or buttermilk, if you can't find kefir. This salad is very forgiving of added extras – try boiled new potatoes, steamed green beans, underripe honeydew melon or an overripe avocado.

Laura loves a barbecue but not for the usual suspects. While she leaves the grill to her partner Paul, she has become rather famous for her sides. And this tomato salad, celebrating the sweet and sour fruit at the height of their season, always makes an appearance.

Serves 4–6 | 10 mins | Vegan

SMOOSHED TOMATO, OLIVE AND BASIL SALAD

Roughly chop **800g ripe, room-temperature heritage tomatoes** (a variety of types, colours and sizes is best) and add to a large bowl. Add **150g pitted and roughly chopped fat green olives**, a large pinch each of flaky sea salt and freshly ground black pepper and, using clean hands, lightly smoosh everything together. Tear in **30g basil leaves**, pour in **5 tbsp extra-virgin olive oil** and **3 tbsp sherry vinegar**. Toss together and leave to sit at room temperature, covered, for at least 20 minutes before serving.

TWIST

Add large crunchy croutons for a salad more akin to a panzanella, toss through hot pasta as a raw tomato sauce, pour over toasted bread rubbed with a small garlic clove to make bruschetta, or serve over fluffy couscous with cubes of halloumi, golden and toasted from dry-frying in a pan.

Traditionally, you might see Thai som tam made with green, (unripe) papaya but the dressing works so well with a multitude of fruit and vegetables. For ultimate flavour, serve immediately while it's crunchy and fresh.

Serves 4–6 | 15 mins

FLAT PEACH AND TURNIP SOM TAM

Whisk together **3 grated garlic cloves, 2–3 tbsp soft brown sugar, 2–3 tbsp fish sauce, 1 sliced red chilli** and the **juice of 4 limes** in a large bowl. Taste and adjust as necessary – you want everything to zing so it's salty, sour, sweet and fiery. Finely shred **2 turnips, 2 carrots** and **2 stoned, unripe flat peaches** into matchsticks. Quarter **125g baby sweetcorn** and **200g trimmed green beans** and halve **250g cherry tomatoes**. Finely slice **3 baby leeks, ¼ iceberg lettuce** and a **handful of coriander leaves**. Add everything to the bowl and toss, before dividing between bowls. Finely chop **65g salted peanuts** and sprinkle over the top.

TWIST

This salad is seriously good on its own, but a 'black and blue' steak, seared over a high heat and sliced rare works wonders, too. Don't have turnips? Try swede, mooli or kohlrabi. Can't find flat peaches? Try unripe nectarines.

Every Christmas day, Laura's nan Gloria would make the whole family a prawn cocktail to start – even though Gloria didn't like prawn cocktail herself. This bowl borrows its spices from another favourite of Laura's – a Bloody Mary cocktail.

Serves 2 | 40 mins

PRAWN COCKTAIL GRAIN BOWL

Put **200g brown rice**, **500g water**, **500g passata**, **½ tsp celery salt**, **½ tsp ground white pepper** and **1 tsp fennel seeds** into a large pan over a medium heat and cook for 30–35 minutes or until the liquid is absorbed and the rice is tender. Meanwhile, chop a **thumb of cucumber**, **2 small handfuls of cherry tomatoes**, **1 avocado**, and thinly slice **½ fennel bulb**. When the rice is cooked, stir in **1 tsp Worcestershire sauce** and **1 tsp sherry** or **red wine vinegar**. Spoon into bowls, top with the chopped veg and **150g cooked prawns**. Squeeze the juice from **½ lemon** over each serving and a **dash of hot sauce** or a **sprinkle of chilli flakes** if you like your Mary spicy!

TIP

Cooking prawns yourself avoids them becoming rubbery - steam raw prawns on top of the rice in a bamboo steamer for the final 3–4 minutes of cooking.

When that woozy combination of warm, summer sunshine and weekend evening strikes, life really does feel golden. Especially if you have an easy three-ingredient cocktail in your hand and some crisp, salty snacks. The same could be said of autumn evenings gathered around an open fire after a long, wind-buffeted walk. With these ideas for drinks (boozy and alcohol-free, hot and cold) and bites to savour during that precious pre-dinner gap you can conjure up that gilded mood on any day.

Choose whichever pink lemonade you like most: some are cloudy while some are clear, some are plain lemonade tinted with food colouring, others are rose- or raspberry-flavoured. The big rule is to avoid anything with synthetic flavourings or artificial sweetener; it won't taste as good.

For crisp and lacy bites, rather than thick and chewy ones, choose Parmesan or Grana Padano and spread the grated cheese on the baking tray as sparsely as you dare. We love nigella seeds; they're pretty to look at and the aromatic, oniony bite balances out the richness of the cheese.

Serves 6 | 5 mins

CHAMPADE

Divide a **75cl bottle of pink lemonade** between six champagne glasses (it should come roughly two-thirds of the way up) then top up the final third of the glasses with **sparkling wine** (this will use roughly half a bottle so buy an extra bottle of lemonade and you'll have enough for a second glass each). Float a fresh **raspberry** on the top of each one and clink away.

Makes around 15 | 10 mins

SPECKLED CHEESE CRISPS

Heat the oven to 180°C fan/200°C/400°F/gas mark 6. Grate **50g Parmesan** or **Grana Padano**, then spread out the cheese in a thin layer across a greaseproof paper-lined baking sheet. Sprinkle **1–2 tsp nigella seeds** across the top. Bake in the oven for 6 minutes, then remove and use a knife to score the molten cheese with rectangular indentations – this will help you to snap it into pieces once cool enough to handle. Lie the snapped crisps on kitchen paper and pat off any remaining oil.

TWIST

If you're not wild about raspberry or rose flavourings, swap out the pink lemonade for elderflower pressé and spear with a sprig of thyme instead of the raspberry.

TIP

If you're a stickler for round crisps, you can spoon the cheese in tablespoons onto the baking sheet. Make sure you leave a gap of 5cm or so between them to allow for spreading.

The vodka-based cousin of a caipirinha – the national cocktail of Brazil – this cocktail is made with vodka, lime and a secret ingredient: raspberry jam, which adds a fruity sweetness.

Laura became rather partial to a lockdown libation to signal the end of the working day during the peak of the pandemic. This margarita, made with often-discarded coriander stems, was crowned the best.

Serves 1 | 5 mins

RASPBERRY CAIPIROSKA

Top and tail **1 lime**, quarter it, cut each quarter in two, and throw all the pieces into a cocktail shaker or large lidded jam jar. Muddle with a wooden spoon, or the end of a rolling pin, then add **2 tsp high-fruit raspberry jam** and **8 ice cubes**. Add **25ml vodka**, put on the lid and shake well, then pour the lot into a glass and sip.

Serves 1 | 5 mins

HERB GARDEN MARGARITA

Add a **handful of ice** to a cocktail shaker or large lidded jam jar. Put **45ml tequila (reposado or blanco)**, the **juice of 1 lime** and **30ml Cointreau** in the shaker with **1–2 chopped pickled chillies**, 1 tsp of the pickled chilli brine and a **small handful of coriander stems and leaves**. Close the lid of the shaker or jam jar and shake until cold. Rub the juiced lime half around the rim of your glass and dip into **1 tsp fine chilli salt** spread out on a side plate. Strain the margarita into the rimmed glass.

TWIST

For a fruity caipirinha, try a St Clements – use any kind of high-fruit marmalade (lime, grapefruit or Seville orange all work well as long as they're fine-cut) in place of the jam and swap vodka for cachaça. The flecks of peel look pretty in the glass.

TWIST

For a grassier frozen mix, blend all the ingredients with a handful of ice, rather than shaking. This makes enough for two glasses, rather than one.

A soothing winter warmer, this hot, spiced orange drink is a comforting way to pack in a shot of vitamin C. It's great to sip around a campfire or bonfire, or to carry in a flask to sip on a walk.

Spiking cocoa with any sweet, flavoured vodka perfumes the drink without overpowering the chocolate. For a more unusual, lokum-like twist we've gone for rose vodka.

Serves 1 | 5 mins

FIRELIGHT

Put **200ml water**, **1 tbsp honey**, **¼ tsp ground turmeric**, **1 cinnamon stick**, a **slice of ginger** and the **juice of 2 blood oranges** in a pan and slowly heat. When hot, strain into a mug, then stir in **3 tbsp ginger wine** and serve with a **star anise** floating on top.

Serves 2 | 10 mins

TURKISH DELIGHT COCOA

Put **2 tbsp cocoa powder** and **1 tbsp caster sugar** in a pan and bash out any lumps. Place the pan over a low-medium heat and measure out **250ml whole milk** or **oat milk** then add to the pan gradually, starting with just 2 tbsp, whisking as you go, adding the rest when the cocoa and sugar have dissolved. Whisk until hot then pour into two cups, stir **2 tbsp rose vodka** into each one and dust them with cocoa powder.

TWIST

If you don't have blood oranges, use normal oranges or lemons. Not a fan of ginger wine? Try 2 tbsp whisky or spiced rum instead, or skip the alcohol altogether if you prefer.

TWIST

If you're not a fan of vodka, try 2 tbsp spiced rum instead. For a non-alcoholic version, replace the rose vodka with ½ tsp rose water.

This lightly spiced cauliflower dish is a multi-tasking all-rounder. Try it as a side to dals (see Veg Box Grater Dal, p78) and curries, or barbecued meats; in a warm wrap with yogurt-mint sauce, or on mini poppadoms as a bite-sized canapé.

Serves 4 as a side dish, 2 as a main | 30 mins | Veggie

TANDOORI CAULIFLOWER BITES

Heat the oven to 180°C fan/200°C/400°F/gas mark 6. Cut **1 head of cauliflower** into very small florets. Whisk together **2 tbsp crunchy peanut butter** (cashew or almond also work), **2 tbsp vegetable oil**, **2 tbsp water**, the **juice of 1 lemon**, **1 tbsp tandoori spice mix** (or garam masala), **1 tbsp desiccated coconut** and a pinch of salt in a large bowl then tip in the florets and coat well. Place the florets on a baking tray, in a single layer, and roast for 25 minutes or until brown on top and tender inside. Meanwhile, put **100g Greek yogurt** in a bowl and stir through **½ tbsp ready-made mint sauce** and a generous pinch of salt to make a dipping sauce.

TWIST

Make your own mint sauce by mixing 8 finely chopped mint leaves, ¼ tsp sugar, ½ tsp lime juice and a pinch of salt into the Greek yogurt (for a looser sauce, add 1–2 tablespoons lime juice). For a dairy-free dip, blitz 50g coriander, 50g mint, 1 tsp granulated sugar, 1 green chilli, the juice of 1 lime and salt in a blender.

Pizza-like pissaladière is a regular on summer lunch or picnic menus for good reason. While we love the original, one major benefit of this pint-sized version is that it works so well as a quick canapé to serve with a drink.

Makes 8 | 20 mins

PISSALADIÈRE CROSTINI

Heat the oven to 170°C fan/190°C/375°F/gas mark 5. Melt a **knob of butter** in a pan over a low-medium heat. Finely slice **2 onions** and fry them in the butter, stirring often, with a **pinch of sugar** and a **slosh of sherry** (optional) for 10 minutes, or until the onions are translucent. Cut **8 x 1cm slices from a baguette** (staler bread is preferable) and place on a baking sheet. Drain the oil from a **30g can of anchovies** into a bowl and use it to lightly brush each side of each slice of baguette. Bake in the oven for 10 minutes, turning the slices halfway through. When cooked, divide the onions, the can of anchovies and **8 pitted black olives** and some **thyme leaves** between the slices.

TWIST

Stick with the Nissarde theme and try a Niçoise salad in crostini form, topping each toast with a spoon of tuna pâté (or mashed, seasoned tuna in oil), ½ a boiled egg (cut-side up), a sun-dried tomato, a single blanched green bean and a chopped black olive.

TIP

Let the nuts cool
completely before
eating. Try them too
soon and they won't
have that crunch.

Here, gentle aromatics from gin and herbaceous rosemary cosy up to the sharp sweetness of ruby grapefruit. And, if you have a floral honey, like British heather, even better.

Salty, crunchy, herby nuts go so well with a drink. We've gone with a mix of parsley, sage, rosemary and thyme – not just because we like the Simon & Garfunkel song but because they work together really well. You don't have to use all four of them.

Serves 1 | 5 mins

BLUSHING GREYHOUND

Add a handful of ice to a cocktail shaker or large lidded jam jar. Add the juice of **½ ruby** or **red grapefruit** (about 80ml), **1 tsp honey, 40ml London dry gin** and a **sprig of rosemary**. Close the lid of the shaker or jar and shake until cold. Strain over fresh ice in a short tumbler and serve with a sprig of rosemary.

Serves 4 | 20 mins | Vegan

SCARBOROUGH FAIR NUTS

Heat the oven to 180°C fan/200°C/400°F/ gas mark 6. Put **1 tbsp olive oil** in a bowl with **3 tsp sea salt**, black pepper and **2 tbsp finely chopped fresh herbs** (a mix of parsley, sage, rosemary and thyme) plus **2 tsp dried herbs** (rosemary and thyme) and mix. Toss in **200g raw mixed nuts** and coat them in the oil, then spread them out in a single layer on a baking tray and roast for 10–15 minutes, stirring halfway through. Leave to cool.

TWIST

Make this alcohol-free by replacing the gin with an alcohol-free spirit, or skip the spirit altogether and pour the sweetened, herby grapefruit juice over ice in a short tumbler. Top with a sprig of rosemary and ginger ale (about 80ml).

TWIST

If your home turns into a pumpkin-carving factory at Halloween, swap in pumpkin seeds instead. Alternatively, try a sweet mix made with maple syrup, ground cinnamon and vanilla paste, or a sweet-salty one with maple syrup, sea salt and rosemary. Roast any syrupy mix on baking paper, to stop the nuts from sticking to the tray.

These colourful, crowd-pleasing poppadoms don't last long under all the delicious chutneys, so curate and serve straightaway. Napkins are a must.

Serves 4 as a snack | 10 mins | Vegan

RAINBOW POPPADOMS

Tip a **large packet (82.5g) of poppadom crisps** (plain or flavoured) or 8 poppadoms smashed into shards onto a platter. Combine **8 tbsp coconut yogurt** with the **juice of 1 lime** in a small bowl. Drizzle over the poppadoms, along with **2–3 tbsp tamarind chutney** and/or **mango chutney** (if they are too thick you can loosen with a little boiling water). Top with the seeds of **1 pomegranate**, a **finely diced shallot**, a **handful of chopped coriander** and a **couple of handfuls of Bombay mix**.

TWIST

Serve alongside the Tandoori Cauliflower Bites (see p131), and if you'd made the coriander chutney too, be sure to drizzle some over the poppadoms.

TIP

Larger ice cubes
are best for shaking
cocktails, as they melt
more slowly and dilute
your drink less.

The dark sweetness and subtle spiciness of blackcurrants is magical with the roasted bitterness of coffee.

Perhaps the most low-effort yet most decadent canapé you'll ever have the pleasure of tasting. If you've never tried this combination before, now is the time.

Serves 1 | 5 mins

BLACKCURRANT ESPRESSO MARTINI

Add a handful of ice to a cocktail shaker or large lidded jam jar. Add **20ml cassis, 20ml coffee liqueur** and **45ml freshly brewed espresso**. Close the lid of the shaker or jam jar and shake until cold. Open the shaker – the drink should look frothy and creamy – and strain into a martini glass.

Serves 4 | 5 mins

CRISPS AND CAVIAR

Take a **150g bag of posh salted crisps** and tip into the fanciest serving bowl you own. Scoop **200ml thick crème fraîche** into another small fancy serving bowl. Finally, open a **jar of caviar** (we're partial to the affordable lumpfish variety). Provide spoons and let guests construct their own perfect mouthful.

TWIST

Add the cassis and coffee liqueur to hot coffee and top with a layer of lightly whipped double cream for an Irish-style coffee.

TWIST

Boil 1kg baby new potatoes or Jersey Royals for 15 minutes. Heat the oven to 180°C fan/200°C/400°F/gas mark 6. Drain the potatoes, tip into a baking tin, drizzle with 2 tbsp extra-virgin olive oil, 1 tbsp dried herbs and salt. Roast for 30-40 minutes until golden and crisp on the outside and fluffy on the inside. Serve split, topped with spoonfuls of crème fraiche and caviar.

Even those of us who don't have a seriously sweet tooth crave the occasional bit of sweetness. You don't need to have expert knowledge or spend hours in the kitchen to rustle up these foolproof, one-paragraph recipes, whether you're after an easy weekday bake, a one-bite pudding or a show-stopping dessert.

Our twist on a simple drizzle cake, this raspberry-weeping loaf bake is full of good, cheering things. Sure to hit a comforting note, whether you're making it as a gift, for a gathering or as an after-school treat.

Serves 10 | 1 hr 20 mins

Heat the oven to 160°C fan/180°C/350°F/gas mark 4. Grease and line a 900g loaf tin. Put **175g softened butter**, **175g golden caster sugar**, **50g ground almonds**, **3 medium eggs**, **1 tbsp whole milk**, **1 tsp vanilla paste** and **175g self-raising flour** into a large bowl and combine with an electric whisk. Pour one-third of the mix into the loaf tin, scatter **50g raspberries** over the top, cover with another third of the cake batter, and **another 50g raspberries**, then pour in the remaining batter and gently smooth over. Bake for 45–65 minutes or until golden on top and a skewer inserted into the cake comes out clean, then remove from the oven. Meanwhile, mash **50g raspberries** through a sieve into a jug. Add the **juice of 1 large lemon** (2 if you like a thinner consistency and a sharper flavour) and **50g icing sugar** and stir. When the cake has cooled slightly, skewer some holes in it then spoon over the drizzle. Remove from the tin when completely cool and scatter a **final 50g raspberries** on top.

TWIST

To make raspberry and almond muffins instead, line a 12-hole muffin tin with cases then divide half the batter among the cases. Scatter a couple of raspberries in each case then spoon in the remaining batter. Pop another raspberry on top of each one and bake for 25 minutes at 160°C fan/180°C/350°F/gas mark 4.

SOMETHING SWEET

Similar in flavour to Bananas Foster, only without the booze, this banana 'ice cream' is best made with ripe – even overripe – bananas. It's easy enough to make your own Ginger Biscuits (see p161) but many of the big-brand ginger biscuits are dairy-free if you want to keep it vegan.

Serves 4 | 15 mins + freezing

FIRE AND SPICE BANANAS

Slice **4 very ripe bananas** into thick coins and freeze for 3 hours. Just before the freeze time is up, slice **another 2 bananas** and roll in **4 tbsp granulated sugar** mixed with ½ **tsp ground cinnamon**. Lightly grease a frying pan with **butter** or **coconut oil**, place over a medium heat and fry the sugar-coated banana coins for a few minutes on each side or until caramelized. Take the pan off the heat. Place the frozen bananas in a food processor with **2 crumbled ginger biscuits** and blitz until smooth – if needed, add a **splash of milk** to help it come together. Spoon the banana 'ice cream' into bowls and top with the caramelized banana and some more crumbled biscuits.

TWIST

Turn this chilly treat into a hot one by placing 4 bananas on a barbecue (you can also oven bake them at 130°C fan/150°C/300°F/gas mark 2 for 15–30 minutes) and cook them for 5 minutes on each side. When they're completely brown all over cut a slit down them lengthways and crumble a ginger biscuit into each one. Spoon the gingery banana directly from the skin, once it's cooled slightly.

If you're cooking dinner in the oven make the most of that heat to make this easy chocolate pud. You can easily scale it up (simply multiply the ingredients by two, four or eight), or freeze it (cook straight from frozen for 2 minutes longer).

Serves 1 | 12 mins | Vegan

12-MINUTE MOLTEN MINT CHOC PUD

Heat the oven to 180°C fan/200°C/400°F/gas mark 6. Mix **2 tbsp golden caster sugar**, **1 tbsp cocoa powder**, **1½ tbsp plain flour**, a teeny pinch of fine salt, **⅛ tsp baking powder**, **⅛ tsp bicarbonate of soda**, **¼ tsp peppermint extract** (optional), **1 tbsp groundnut oil** and **3 tbsp oat milk** in a jug or mug until smooth. Lightly brush a dariole mould with **¼ tsp groundnut oil** then dust with **1–2 tsp cocoa powder** and turn the mould around until fully coated. Pour in the batter, add a **chocolate truffle**. Bake for 10–12 minutes, or until just set. Carefully tease around the edge with a table or palette knife. Place a plate on top, quickly invert and turn out the pudding.

TIP

If you don't have a dariole mould, bake in a deep muffin tin and pour the mix into it until it just covers the truffle. Bake for 10-12 minutes, or until just set, then leave for two minutes before gently teasing out with a knife. Of course it's more difficult to turn out multiple puds cleanly from a muffin tin so this method is easier when you're just making two

TWIST

Try other flavourings –
rose water and white
chocolate truffles,
Frangelico and pralines
or orange blossom water
and chocolate orange.

Our quick and easy stovetop rice pudding is pure comfort in a bowl. Go against the grain and try it for a warming weekend breakfast in winter.

Serves 4 | 1 hr 10 mins

STOVETOP RICE PUDDINGS

MARMALADE RICE PUDDING

Put **40g golden caster sugar, 850ml whole milk** and **1 tsp orange blossom water** in a heavy-based pan and bring to a simmer. Turn the heat down, tip in **100g pudding rice** and simmer gently for around an hour, stirring regularly, until creamy and tender. Serve with a **generous dollop of Seville orange marmalade**.

SPICED RICE PUDDING

Put **40g golden caster sugar, 850ml whole milk** and **2 tsp mixed spice** (anything with the masala chai spices – cinnamon, cardamom, ginger and cloves – plus nutmeg is good) in a heavy-based pan and bring to a simmer. Turn the heat down, tip in **100g pudding rice** and simmer gently for around an hour, stirring regularly, until creamy and tender.

One of the best things about this recipe is the delicious way it makes your home smell. The recipe title nods not to when you should be eating them but to two different sauces the pears go brilliantly with. Cover them with a rich cloak of molten chocolate, or top them with creamy, cardamom-flecked yogurt.

Serves 4 | 35 mins

NIGHT AND DAY PEARS

Heat the oven to 160°C fan/180°C/350°F/gas mark 4. Mix **2 tbsp softened salted butter** with **1 tsp brown sugar** and finely crushed seeds from a small **cardamom pod**. Halve and core **2 ripe pears** and fill the holes with the spiced butter. Sprinkle a little more brown sugar over the pears then bake for 25 minutes. Meanwhile, make your sauce (see below). Serve with the pears and their buttery juices.

SALTED CHOCOLATE SAUCE

While the pears are baking, mix **5 tbsp cocoa powder** and **10 tbsp caster sugar** in a pan, bashing out any lumps with a wooden spoon. Add **5 tbsp water**, stir and gently bring to the boil. Simmer for a minute, then take off the heat. Let the sauce cool a little to thicken, then stir in a pinch of flaky sea salt and pour over the pears. If you have left over sauce you can always whisk some milk into it, little by little, and heat it up to make cocoa.

CARDAMOM GREEK YOGURT

While the pears are baking, finely crush the seeds of **2 cardamom pods** and stir through **8 tbsp Greek yogurt** along with **1–2 tsp icing sugar** then spoon onto the warm pears.

When you fancy something sweet but not too heavy at the end of a meal, affogato is the answer: hot espresso poured over cold vanilla ice cream. We've taken inspiration from the flavoured syrups in neighbourhood coffee shops to give the classic Italian dessert a freshly brewed twist.

Serves 4 | 5 mins

COFFEE SHOP AFFOGATO

Take **500ml ice cream** out of the freezer to soften slightly. Choose one of the following flavours: vanilla (flat white), chocolate (think mocha latte), cardamom (chai latte), salted caramel (caramel cortado), coffee (double shot espresso), ginger or gingerbread (gingerbread latte) or cinnamon (cinnamon-spiced cappuccino). Make **4 espressos** (if you don't have an espresso machine just make a rich, stronger-than-usual brew of coffee in a cafetière). Scoop 2 balls of the ice cream into four shatterproof tumblers, coffee cups or bowls and quickly pour about 30ml of hot coffee over each serving.

TIP

If you're making this for more than four, the ice cream might melt and the coffee cool, by the time you've served everyone's scoops. For true cold-meets-hot perfection, scrape out scoops of ice cream in advance, laying them on a plastic lid or tray as you go, then put the tray in the freezer until you're ready to serve.

Piña colada cocktails are a sure-fire way to teleport your taste buds to sunnier shores. The trio of tropical flavours also works brilliantly in pudding form – as these mini pavlovas, very moreishly, demonstrate.

Serves 4 | 35 mins

MINI PIÑA COLADA PAVLOVAS

Heat the oven to 180°C fan/200°C/400°F/gas mark 6. Top, tail and peel **1 pineapple**. Cut it into quarters and remove the core. Cut each quarter into about 14 pineapple chunks. Melt **2 tbsp coconut oil** and **2 tbsp sugar** in a small roasting tin on the hob then tip the pineapple into the tin and coat with the oil and sugar. Transfer the tin to the oven and roast for 20 minutes, turning and basting after 10. Take the tin out of the oven and leave the pineapple to cool a little while you put **4 small meringue nests** into four bowls. Whip **200ml double cream** with **2 tbsp rum** and **1 tbsp icing sugar** and divide between the nests. Top with the roasted pineapple, a **scattering of desiccated** or **toasted coconut flakes** and the **zest of 1 lime**.

TWIST

For a simple, alcohol-free piña colada dessert, top coconut yogurt or coconut ice cream with the roasted pineapple, toasted coconut and lime zest.

It's hard not to love this exceptionally simple five-ingredient – and, incidentally, vegan – mousse. Sweetened coconut cream is whipped to billowy clouds and combined with peanut butter and crushed nuts.

Serves 2 | 5 mins + chilling | Vegan

GO NUTS MOUSSE

Open a **400ml can coconut milk** or **coconut cream** and drain the water that has separated from the cream. Freeze this water for another recipe (such as a Thai green curry or the Totally Tropical Smoothie on p28). Scoop the remaining thick cream into a bowl and whip for 30 seconds or until light and fluffy. Whisk in **2–3 tbsp peanut butter** (dark roast, with whole nuts, is best), **1 tbsp icing sugar** and a pinch of flaky sea salt. Scoop into two serving glasses and pop in the fridge for 30 minutes. Serve with **2 tbsp chopped salted peanuts**.

TIP

You want the thick coconut cream and water to be separated, rather than a homogeneous creamy milk. You can often tell this by gently shaking the can – if you can hear the liquid sloshing around, it's not the can for you. You can also experiment with flavoured nut butters.

This chocolate bark is the answer when you just want a one-bite sweet hit at the end of a meal. Ensure you buy 70 percent dark chocolate and above. If you want to make it even speedier, swap the toppings for 65g crushed biscotti biscuits.

Serves 8 | 20 mins + cooling

SALTY-SWEET DARK CHOCOLATE BARK

Melt **200g dark chocolate** in a heatproof bowl set over a pan of gently simmering water, ensuring the base of the bowl isn't touching the water. Stir occasionally. Remove from the heat, stir in **1 tbsp extra-virgin olive oil** and allow to cool for 15 minutes. Pour into a tray lined with baking paper or a silicone mat and use a spatula or palette knife to spread into a rectangle. Sprinkle over **20g salted peanuts, 20g crushed salted pretzels, 20g crushed breadsticks, 5g sweet and salty** or **butterscotch popcorn** and a large pinch of flaky sea salt. Allow to cool completely before snapping into shards.

TIP

Avoid hot days in the kitchen for this one, otherwise the chocolate won't set. You can pop it in the fridge but it will lose its glossy shine.

TWIST

Keep it simple and swap the toppings for 65g crushed biscotti biscuits.

Three-ingredient peanut butter cookies are a classic for good reason, and suit all kinds of different flavourings. They also freeze brilliantly; freeze for an hour after you've placed them on the lined tray, then scoop them up into freezer bags and, when you're ready, cook them straight from frozen (add on an extra minute or two's cooking time).

Makes 20 cookies | 15 mins + chilling and cooling

PICK 'N' MIX PEANUT BUTTER COOKIES

Beat together **260g smooth peanut butter** (flavoured nut butters work well too), **200g golden caster sugar** and **1 medium egg** to form a smooth dough. Heat the oven to 160°C fan/180°C/350°F/gas mark 4. Roll into 20 ping pong-sized balls and place on two lined baking sheets. Use a fork or your thumb to flatten or indent each ball. Bake, a sheet at a time, on the middle shelf for 10–12 minutes or until the cookies are doubled in size and beginning to turn from pale to golden brown. Leave on the tray to firm up and cool completely.

TWIST

Flex the dough by adding 1 tsp ground ginger, to make ginger nuts (ideal for the Fire and Spice Bananas on p145) or add 1 tsp Lebanese seven spice for a grown-up biscuit, perfect with coffee. When it comes to decorating, dip or drizzle in melted chocolate, or add ½ tsp jam to the indents or, while the cookies are warm, sprinkle over finely crushed salted peanuts and gently press to make them stick.

RHIANNON'S 10 ONE-SENTENCE RECIPES

SERVES 2

SCORCHED TOMATOES ON TOAST

Toss **400g cherry vine tomatoes** in a roasting tin with **1½ tbsp olive oil**, a scattering of **fresh thyme**, **salt**, **pepper** and **chilli flakes**, and roast at 180°C fan/200°C/400°F/gas mark 6 for 25 minutes, before spooning onto **toasted sourdough**.

RADISHES WITH CELERY SALT

Arrange **5 radishes** on each of two plates, along with **½ tbsp butter**, **½ tsp celery salt** and a knife; smear a dot of butter on each radish before dipping it in the **celery salt** and enjoying with a glass of crisp sparkling wine.

BAKED CAMEMBERT

Score the top of a **whole camembert**, drizzle with **honey**, **rosemary** and **sea salt**, then wrap in foil and bake at 180°C fan/200°C/400°F/gas mark 6 for 10–12 minutes, before scooping out the cheese with pieces of **warm baguette**.

DATE AND PERSIMMON SALAD

Stone and halve **4 dates** and **slice 2 persimmons**, then divide both between 2 plates, alternating for prettiness. Drizzle each one with **1 tsp honey**, the **juice of ½ lime** and a couple of **raw, cracked cashews**.

CUCUMBER SMØRREBRØD

Spread **150–200g soft goat's cheese** between **4 slices of rye** or sourdough bread and top each slice with **5 thin slices of cucumber,** a pinch of **sea salt** and **½ tsp za'atar** (or more, to taste).

ELDERFLOWER AND PISTACHIO YOGHURT BOWLS

Swirl **1 tbsp elderflower cordial** through **250g Greek yoghurt**, divide between 2 bowls or cups and top with a **handful of raspberries** and a **few chopped pistachios.**

MACKEREL AND BUTTERBEAN SALAD

Mix **2 tbsp apple cider vinegar**, **4 tbsp olive oil**, **salt**, **pepper**, **½ a finely sliced red onion**, **400g butter beans**, **250g halved vine tomatoes**, **50g pitted black olives**, **a handful of chopped flat-leaf parsley** and **150g flaked smoked mackerel** and divide between 2 plates.

MASALA SCRAMBLED EGGS

Fry **2 chopped spring onions**, **½ tsp ground turmeric**, **½ tsp garam masala**, a **pinch of salt** and **¼ tsp chilli flakes** in **1 tbsp butter**, then add **2 diced tomatoes** and cook until soft before stirring in **4 beaten eggs** and a **handful of chopped coriander**; serving with toast.

TIPSY TANGERINES

Dip the cut sides of **3 halved tangerines** in a **little brown sugar**, then sear them, sugar side-down, in a hot, dry pan until bronzed and caramelised, before serving topped with a **splash of Cointreau** and **scoops of vanilla ice cream.**

CARDAMOM MACAROONS

Mix **1 egg white**, **50g caster sugar**, **1 small crushed cardamom pod**, **50g desiccated coconut** and **15g toasted coconut flakes**, shape into six small balls on a lined baking sheet and bake at 160°C fan/180°C/350°F/ gas mark 4 for 12 minutes.

LAURA'S 10 ONE-SENTENCE RECIPES

SERVES 2

NUTTY NOODLES

Whisk **2 tbsp peanut butter**, **1 tbsp sriracha**, **2–3 tsp fish sauce**, **juice from ½ a lime** and **4 tbsp boiling water** and toss with boiled and drained **noodles** and **long-stemmed broccoli**, before topping with **1 tbsp sesame seeds** and **1 sliced spring onion**.

GINGER CUCUMBER SALAD

Whisk **1 tsp white miso paste**, **2 tsp sesame oil**, **2 tsp rice wine vinegar**, **2 tsp chopped pickled ginger**, **1 tsp pickled ginger brine**, a **pinch of salt**, **1 tbsp toasted sesame seeds** and **1 tbsp chopped dill**, and toss through ½ **a chopped cucumber**.

MARMITE POTATO SKINS

Bake **1 large potato** in a 220°C fan/200°C/425°F/gas mark 7 oven for 1 hour, before halving, scooping out the flesh, mashing with **1 tsp Marmite**, a **knob of butter** and **50g grated Cheddar**, and returning to the shells to bake for another another 15-20 minutes.

ANCHOVY CABBAGE SLAW

Mix **8–10 good-quality anchovy fillets** (finely chopped), **3 tbsp olive oil**, **2 tbsp lemon juice** and **1 tsp ground black pepper** with ½ **a shredded white cabbage**.

5-MINUTE KEFIR FLATBREADS

Mix **100g self-raising flour** with **5 tbsp kefir** and **salt**, before gently kneading, rolling until 1cm thick and cooking in a hot, dry frying pan for a few minutes each side.

POSH DOG TRAYBAKE

Chop **1 large smoked Polish sausage**, **250g halloumi**, **1 large potato** and **1 red pepper** into large chunks, toss with oil and roast in a large baking tray at 220°C fan/200°C/425°F/gas mark 7 for 40 minutes.

CRAB SPAGHETTI

Fry ½ **diced fennel bulb**, **1 diced shallot**, ½ **tsp dried chilli flakes** and **salt** in **2 tbsp olive oil** until softened, before stirring in **crabmeat**, a **handful of chopped tarragon**, the **zest and juice of a lemon**, 200g **al dente spaghetti** and a **mug of pasta water**.

BRIOCHE JAFFA JAFFLE

Butter the bottom of **2 slices of brioche**, spread the tops with a **generous layer of chocolate spread** and **marmalade** and top each one with another slice of buttered brioche, before cooking in a toastie machine or in a frying pan until golden and toasted.

I SCREAM FOR SHEZ ICE CREAM

Gently simmer **75g raisins** and **100ml pedro ximenez sherry** for 5 minutes, then pour over balls of **vanilla ice cream**.

FEELIN' FRUITY ICED TEA

Brew a pot of **jasmine tea** and allow to cool, before pouring over ice, **frozen slices of lemon**, **cucumber** and **fresh mint**.

HARD-WORKING RECIPES

Think of this collection of recipes as trusted accessories to your regular 'wardrobe' of meals. They're great for adding crunch, flavour and colour to other dishes, or to get more 'wear' from a single ingredient. We've cross-referenced to this page from recipes throughout the book in which they would make delicious additions or swap-ins but don't stop there. You'll find they come in handy with so many recipes.

DUKKAH

Toast a **handful of nuts** (hazelnuts, walnuts and almonds all work well) in a dry frying pan over a medium heat for 5 minutes or until golden and aromatic. Remove from the pan, **add a handful of seeds** (sunflower, pumpkin and sesame are good) for 2–3 minutes or until they begin to colour and pop before removing to the same bowl as the nuts. Finally, add 2 tsp each of **cumin seeds** and **coriander seeds** and toast for 1–2 minutes until fragrant. Allow everything to cool. Tip into a mortar, along with the nuts and seeds, or the bowl of a processor and pound or pulse until roughly broken up. Store in an airtight jar for up to 2 weeks.

POTLUCK PESTO

Blend **50g walnuts or pumpkin seeds** (ideally toasted), **100g flat-leaf parsley or basil** (if you're a traditionalist), **1 garlic clove**, **½ tsp salt**, **100ml cold-pressed rapeseed oil**, **50g cubed Cheddar** and **1 tbsp water** until you have a smooth green sauce.

DRESSY DRESSING

Add **1 tsp wholegrain** or **dijon mustard**, ½ **tsp salt**, **1 tsp za'atar**, **2 tbsp lemon juice** and **3 tbsp extra virgin olive oil** to a jam jar. Screw on the lid and shake until emulsified. Use to dress **lettuce leaves**, **steamed broccoli**, or **cooked beetroot**.

QUICK-PICKLED ONIONS

Cut **1 onion** (red is prettiest but white onions work too) in half and then into thin slices. Place in a large jam jar and pour over **300ml apple cider vinegar**, **1½ tbsp caster sugar**, ¾ **tbsp salt** and the **juice of a lime**. Stir and leave to marinate. They taste good after a few hours but try to wait 24 if you can. Alternatively, if you have a jar of cornichons simply keep the brine when you've finished the cornichons and re-use it to pickle the onions instead of making your own pickling juice. Generally you can safely re-use pickling brine at least once, sometimes more. A rule of thumb is to check that the liquid is clear: a cloudy brine can indicate bacterial growth. These pickles will keep for weeks in the fridge.

VEGAN SOUR COCKTAILS

Instead of throwing away drained chickpea water pour it into an ice-cube tray and freeze. The cubes work brilliantly shaken into a sour cocktail for a vegan alternative to egg white. For an amaretto sour, add **45ml amaretto**, **30ml lemon juice**, **1 tsp cherry syrup** (from a jar or can of cherries) and **2 frozen cubes of chickpea water** to a cocktail shaker. Add the lid and shake for 30 seconds – the shaker should be cold to touch and you'll no longer hear the cubes clinking. No need to strain, simply pour the fluffy cocktail straight into a fancy-pants glass and enjoy. Want to experiment? Swap the amaretto for whisky or gin; swap the cherry syrup for maple syrup or sugar syrup; or swap the lemon juice for lime.

ACKNOWLEDGEMENTS

I probably should keep my thanks to one paragraph and if I were to do that there really would be only one person I would dedicate this to. This is the person that helped catapult my career in the direction I so craved, giving me my first article in the magazine that I would later edit for five golden years back in 2014. Her writing, editing and determination to find the most entrancing and delicious places to visit around the world have brought me so much joy since I've known her. Her passion and attention to detail have driven me to be better, and when we both were told our roles had been made redundant at the jobs we loved, at the peak of Covid-19, she gave me the confidence to keep going. She also gave me the privilege of sharing this project with her – as *Rustle Up* began in her exceptional brain. So thank you, Rhiannon, for allowing me to be your partner in crime and for giving me hope in my winter.

But of course, there are so many other gems who helped us make our dream a reality. From Jane and Maddy, our agents, for having faith in us. For Sophie, our editor, for trusting us, and giving us the freedom to cook and write as we wanted. (And Stephanie for tidying us up.) To Laura, Clare, Lola, Lauren, Hattie and Georgina for bringing our vision to life with the most beautiful images. The shoots were so much fun – thank you.

And finally, to my family. Mum and dad, thank you for feeding me so well, even when you definitely didn't have the time to do so – and for believing in me, always. Thank you to Rosie for being a constant inspiration, support and source of sunshine. And to Paul – the one I feed and the one I love – thank you for staying hungry.
(And washing up.)

Laura

To paraphrase the old saying about raising children, it takes a village to bring a cookbook to life, and we've been lucky to have an absolute chocolate-box one as our supporting team.

Thank you to Jane Graham-Maw and Maddy Belton at Graham Maw Christie for seeing the potential in our proposal, and in us. I am deeply grateful to Sophie Allen at Pavilion for grasping our idea and running with it, and for her patience, support and good humour along the way. Also to Laura Russell, whose gorgeous book design demonstrates why you should always work with an art director whose surname reflects your book title. Thanks to Stephanie Evans for her fine-toothed proof-reading. And to photographer Clare Winfield for bringing our recipes to life so beautifully, and with so much care. Thanks also to Lola Milne, Hattie Baker and Georgia Miall for bringing their expert food styling skills into play. You were a dream team to work with.

Growing up with parents who modelled an adventurous and open-minded attitude towards eating, and the value of cooking thriftily from scratch, is something I am sincerely grateful for. Thanks also to the many friends and family members (some of them mentioned in this book) whose generous cooking for me over the years has, directly or indirectly, inspired some of these recipes.

My biggest thanks, however, go to Laura Rowe. I had the initial, embryonic idea for this book during a sunny walk in Pembrokeshire, wondering whether I could reduce some of my family's favourite meals to just one paragraph to make them more do-able on a camping trip. My second thought, only fractionally later, was that I should talk to Laura about coming in with me and developing the idea. Calm, focused, smart and kind, there are few people so committed to food, or so adept at unravelling the mysteries behind it. I also knew first-hand what a skilled and collaborative writer and editor she is. This book quite literally wouldn't be half what it is without her.

Finally, Richard, Osian and Owen, this book is for you! Thank you for being such uncomplaining, adventurous eaters, and for always making me smile. I would happily cook 100-paragraph meals if it meant I got to sit around a table with you.

Rhiannon

INDEX

INDEX

172